LESSON BOOK

B

PIANO Adventures®
by Nancy and Randall Faber
A BASIC PIANO METHOD

CONTENTS

Unit 1 The Family of C's 2

Unit 2 Cross-Hand Arpeggios 6

Unit 3 The Sixth 10

Unit 4 The C Major Scale 14

Unit 5 The G Major Scale 22

Unit 6 More About the Damper Pedal . 30

Unit 7 The Eighth Rest 36

Unit 8 The Dotted Quarter Note 38

Unit 9 The IV Chord 42

Unit 10 The F Major Scale 50

Production: Frank and Gail Hackinson
Production Coordinator: Marilyn Cole
Editors: Victoria McArthur and Edwin McLean
Cover and Illustrations: Terpstra Design, San Francisco
Engraving: GrayBear Music Company, Hollywood, Florida

ISBN 978-1-61677-084-6

Copyright © 1994 by Dovetree Productions, Inc. (ASCAP).
This Edition © 1997 by Dovetree Productions, Inc. (ASCAP).
c/o FABER PIANO ADVENTURES, 3042 Creek Dr., Ann Arbor, MI 48108
International Copyright Secured.   All Rights Reserved.   Printed in U.S.A.
WARNING: The music, text, design, and graphics in this publication are protected by copyright law.
Any duplication is an infringement of U.S. copyright law.

The Family of C's

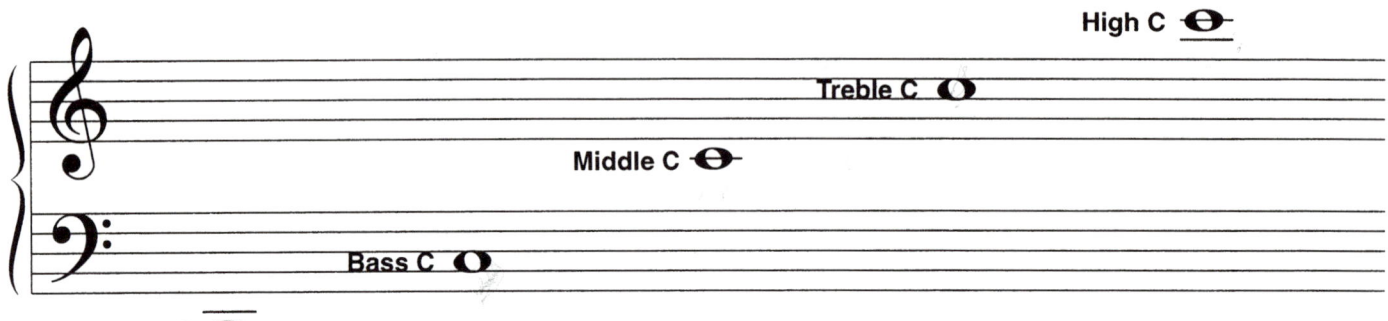

A **ledger line** is a short line added above or below the staff for notes that are too high or too low to be written on the staff.

LOW C is located 2 ledger lines *below* the bass clef staff.
HIGH C is located 2 ledger lines *above* the treble clef staff.

Play each C above on the piano saying its correct name aloud.
(Use finger 3 for each hand.)

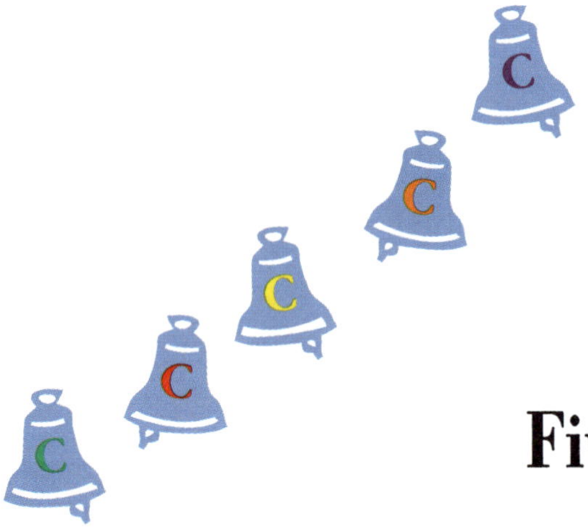

Five Bells

For a ringing bell sound, use the weight of your arm to "drop into" each key.

Slowly, majestically

f

Pedal down.   *Lift pedal.*

 Can you play this piece counting aloud "1 - 2 - 3 - 4"?

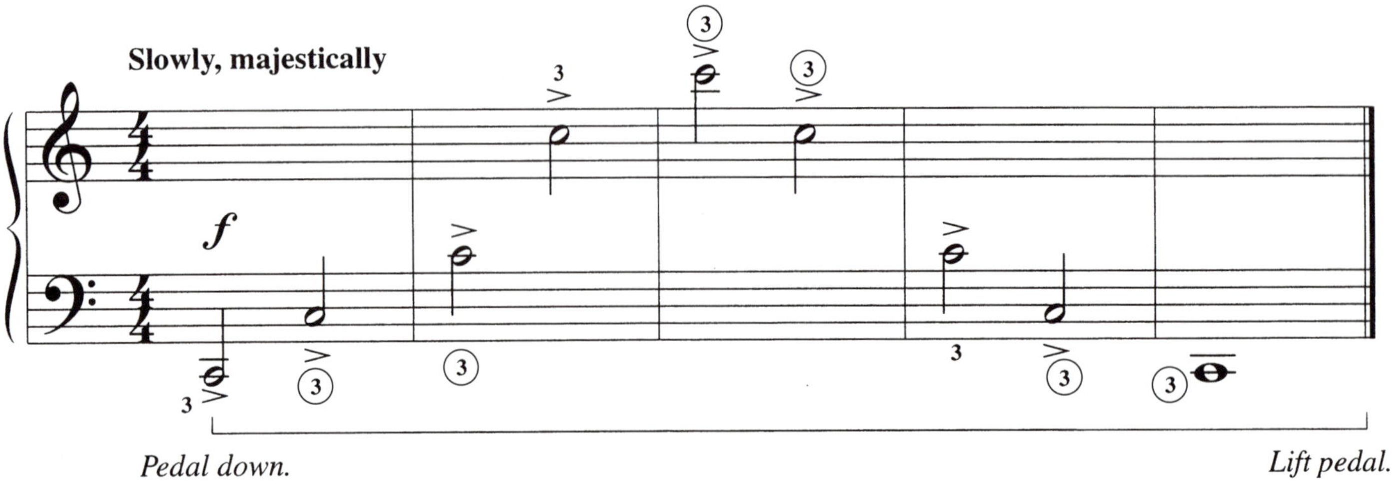

Technique p.2 Heavy Arms

Practice Hint:

First learn *measures 5-8*. These measures use only notes from the C chord.

Cathedral Chimes

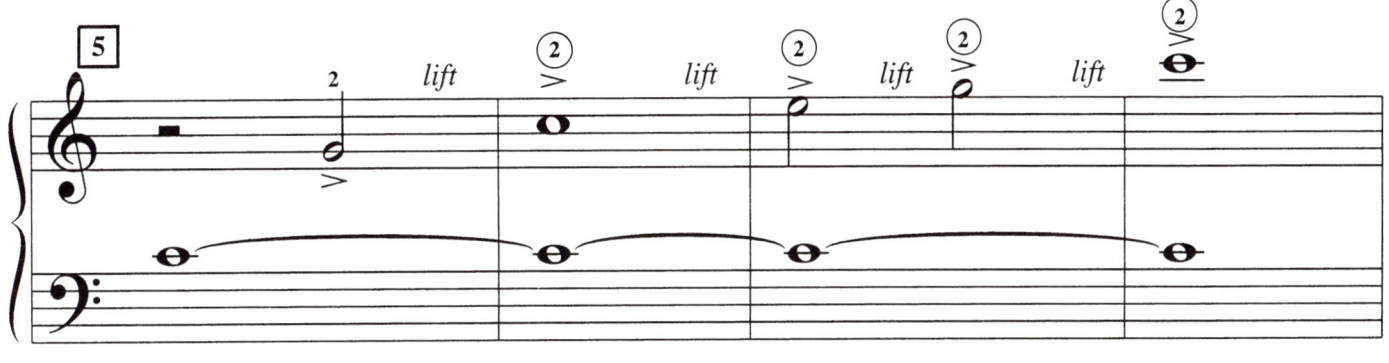

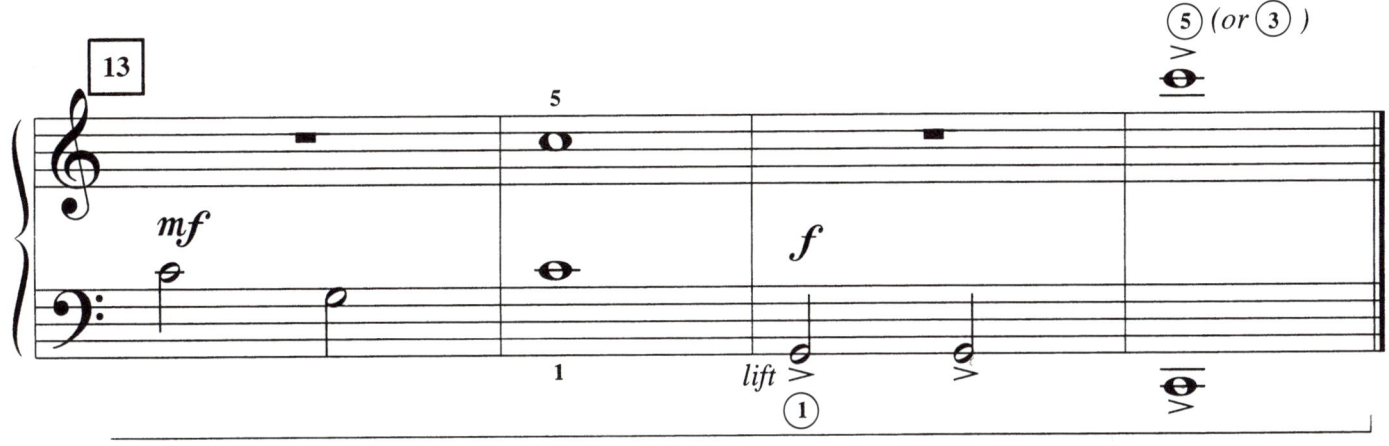

Review: This sign 𝄐 is a ***fermata***.
It means to hold this note longer than usual.

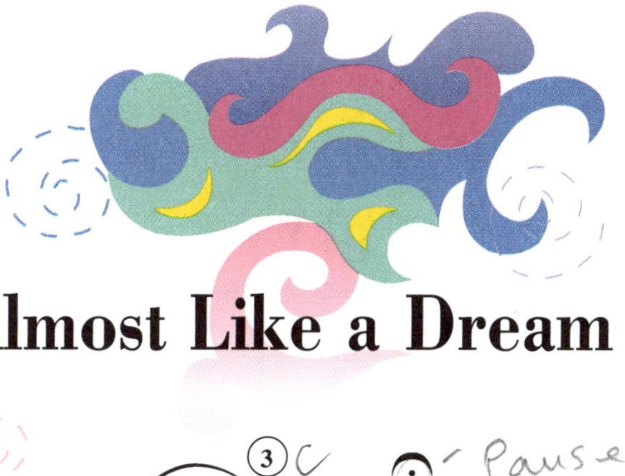

Almost Like a Dream

Andante (walking speed, ♩ = 66-72)

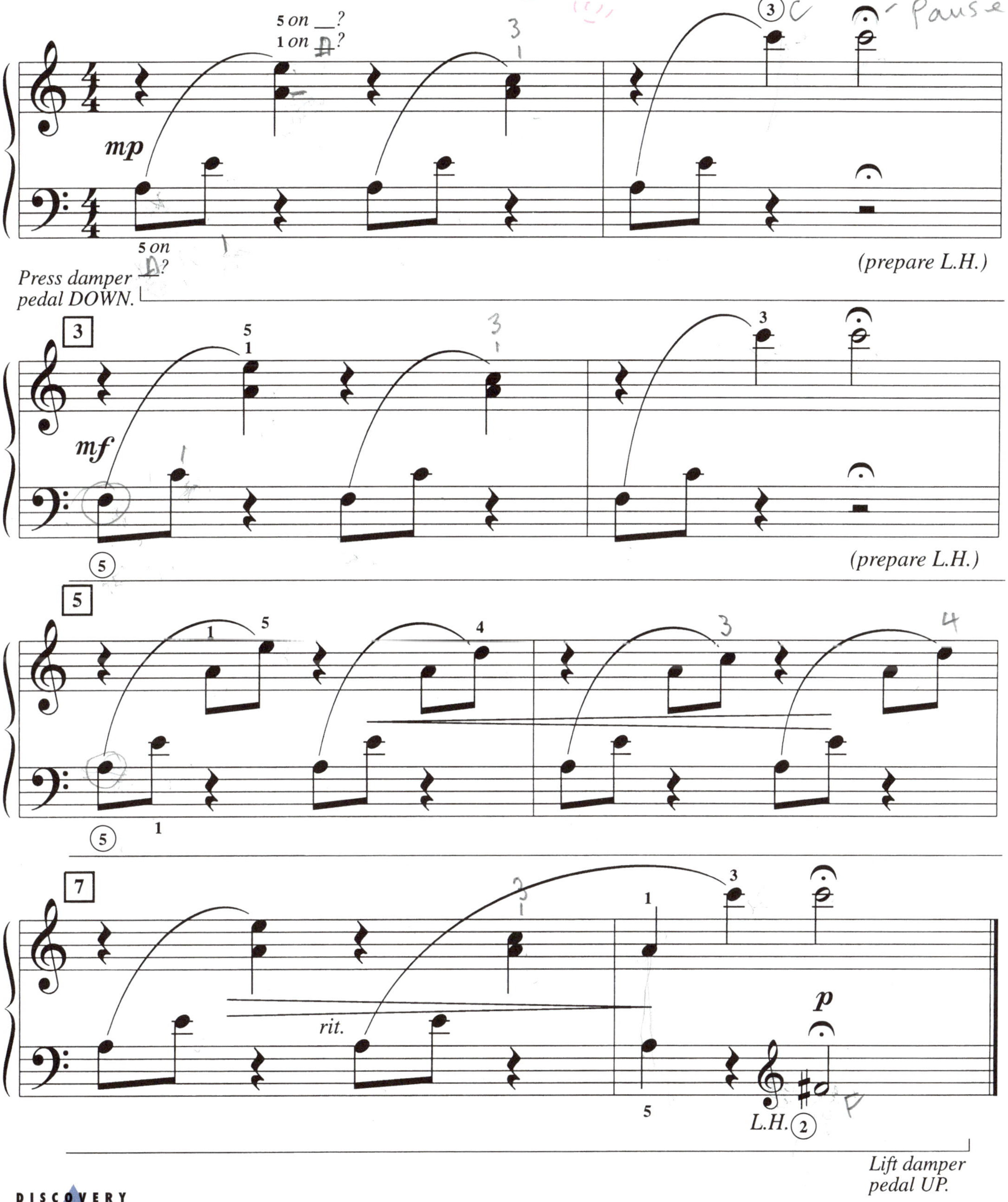
5 on __?
1 on __?
mp
5 on __?
Press damper pedal DOWN.
(prepare L.H.)
mf
(prepare L.H.)
rit.
p
L.H.
Lift damper pedal UP.

Technique p. 2 *Painter's Brush Stroke*, p. 6, 7

DISCOVERY

Is the starting position in this piece **A major** or **A minor**? (circle one)

Cross-Hand Arpeggios

Arpeggio comes from the Italian word for "harp." Your teacher will help you pronounce it.
To play an *arpeggio*, play the notes of a chord one after another going up or down the keyboard.

Practice these major and minor cross-hand arpeggios until you can play them smoothly and easily.

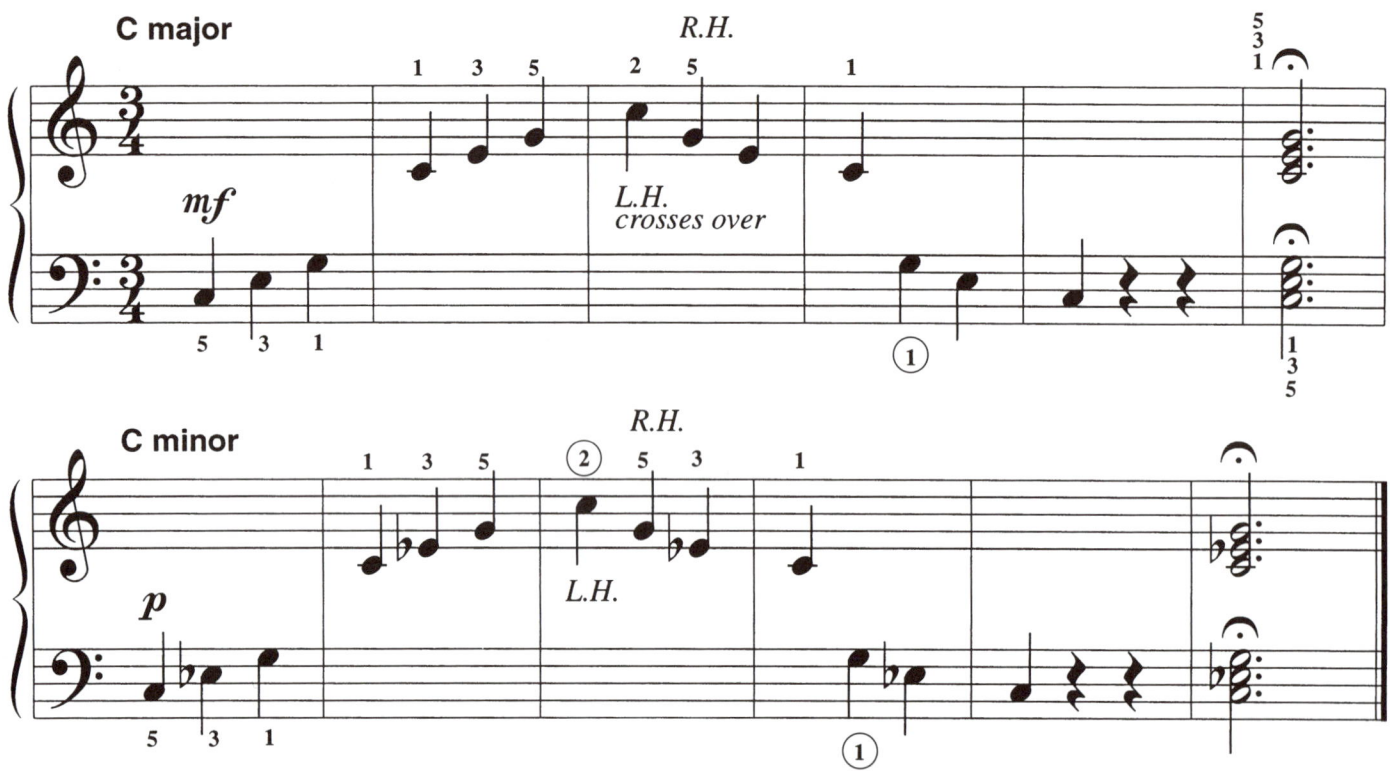

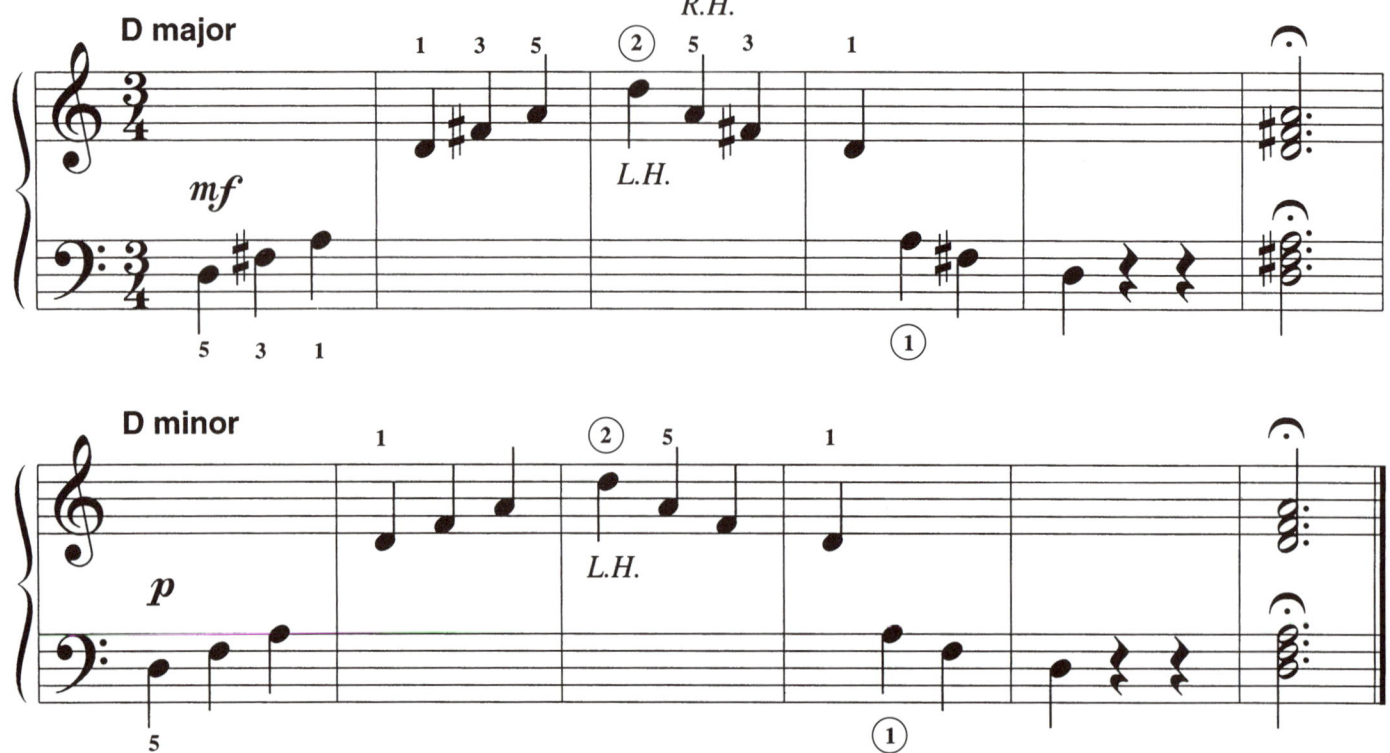

E major

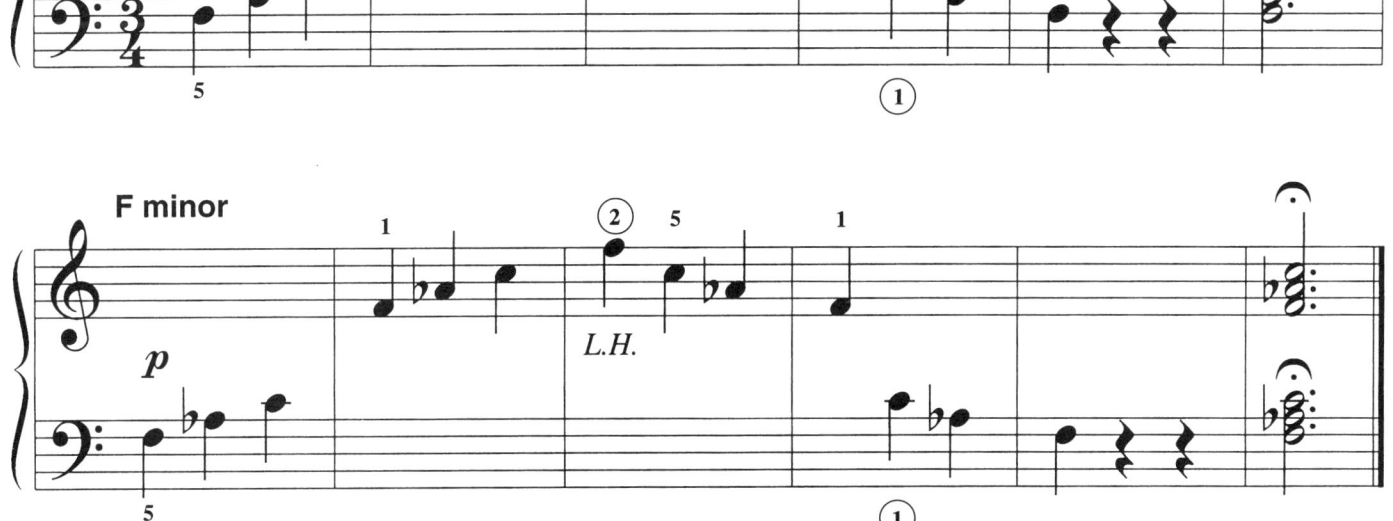

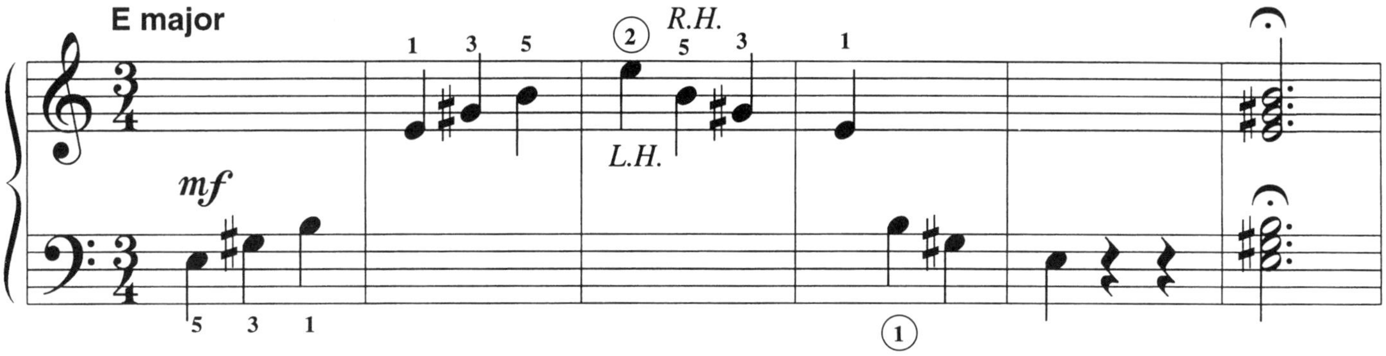

E minor

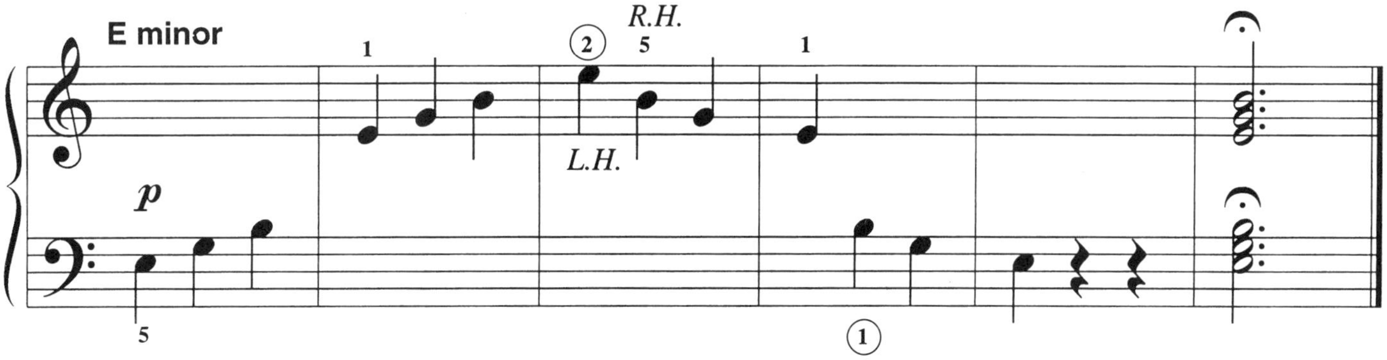

F major

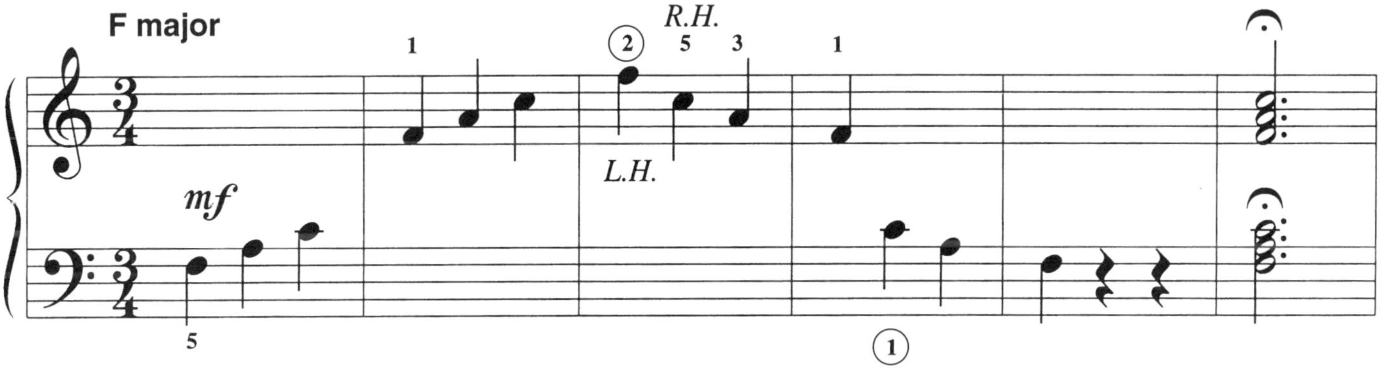

F minor

Play cross-hand arpeggios in G major and G minor, A major and A minor.

Teacher note: It is recommended that the student gradually learn cross-hand arpeggios in all 12 keys.
For a complete listing of all 12 major and minor cross-hand arpeggios, see:
Achievement Skill Sheet #1, Major 5-finger Patterns and Cross-Hand Arpeggios AS5001
Achievement Skill Sheet #2, Minor 5-finger Patterns and Cross-Hand Arpeggios AS5002

Spanish Caballero*

Allegro (♩ = 126-138)

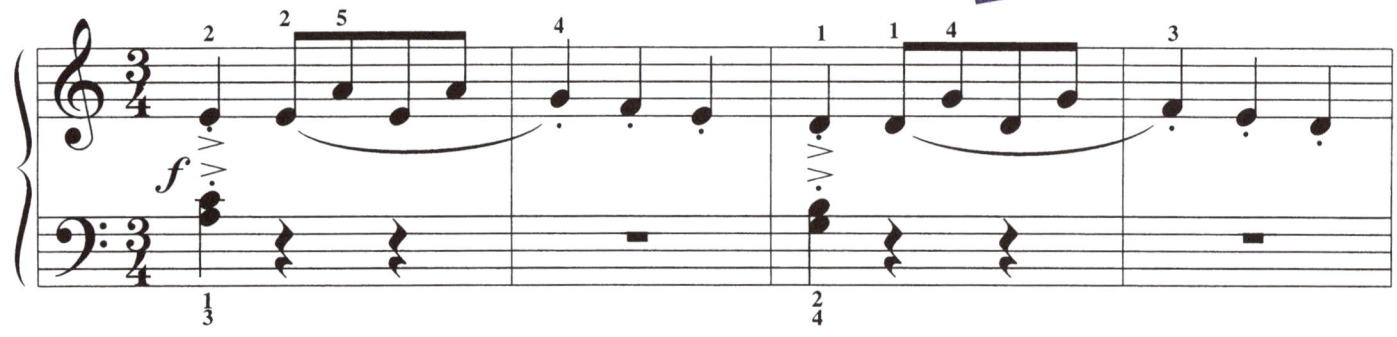

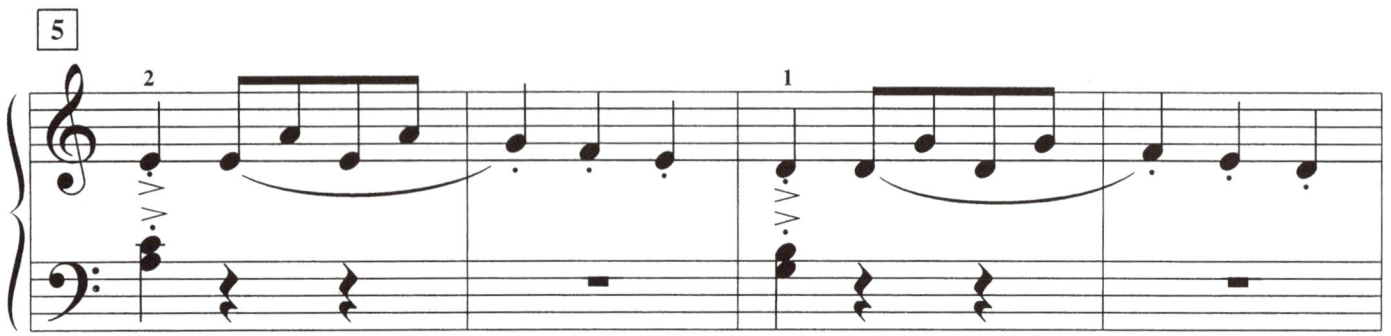

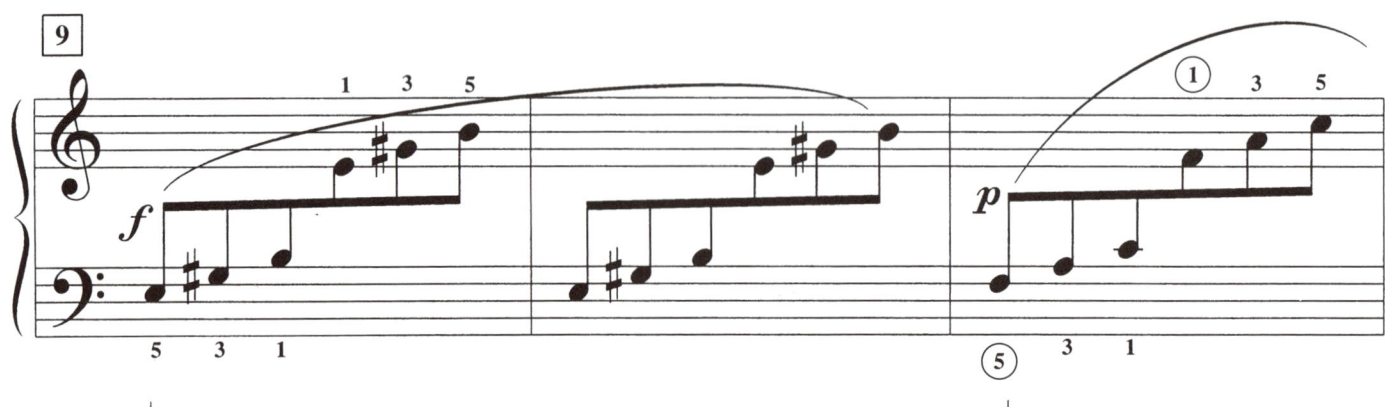

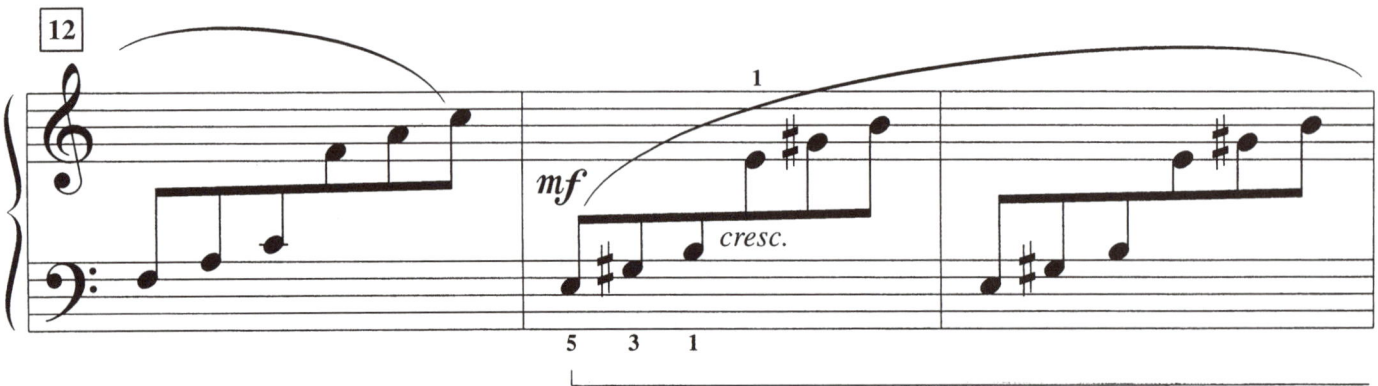

* *caballero* (kah-bah-YEH-roh) — a Spanish horseman

Compose a short piece that uses cross-hand arpeggios.
Call it "The Flight of the Eagle" or a title of your choice.

UNIT 3

Sixth (6th)

Review: An interval is the distance between 2 notes on the keyboard or staff.

New: The interval of a 6th covers 6 keys and 6 letter names.
Write the correct letter name on each keyboard below.

Ex.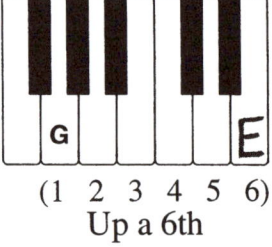
(1 2 3 4 5 6)
Up a 6th

Up a 6th

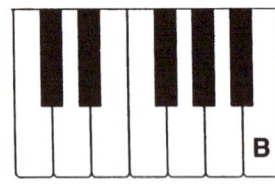
Down a 6th

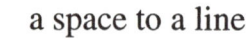
Down a 6th

Now find and play the 6ths above on the piano.
Play the notes separately, then together. Use either hand.

On the staff, a 6th is:

     a line to a space   or   a space to a line

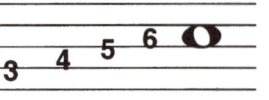   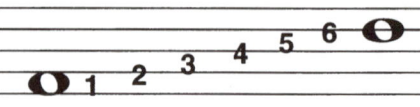

Sixth Hour

DISCOVERY

Remember, playing the same music in a new position is called *transposing*.

Play *Sixth Hour* with the R.H. beginning on  and L.H. on

Boxcar Rumble

Rhythm Check: Play each hand alone as a warm-up.
Can you play this piece while counting aloud "1-2-3-4"?

DISCOVERY Circle three intervals below that are a **line to a space** or a **space to a line**.

2nd   3rd   4th   5th   6th

Teacher Duet: (Student plays as written)

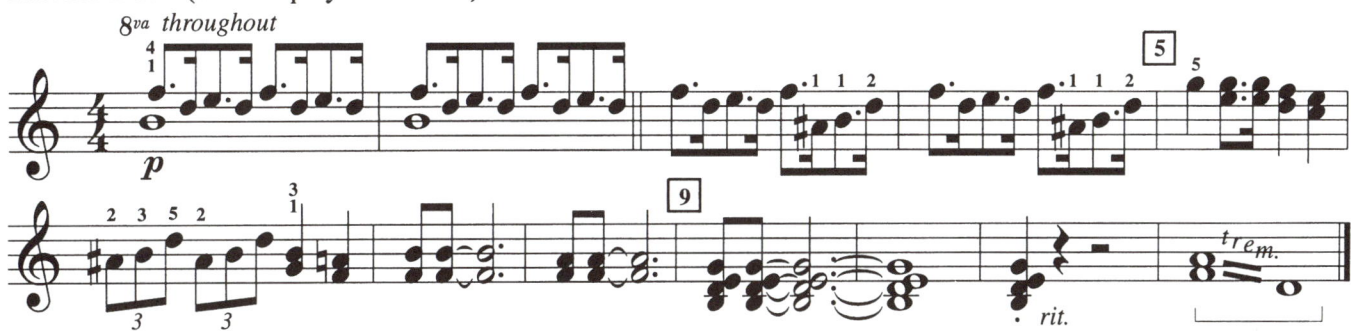

In the armed forces, taps are played as a signal for lights out, everyone to bed.

Listen to the restful sound of **6ths** in this piece.

This piece is written entirely for the LEFT HAND.

Your left hand will play the bass and treble notes!

Warm-up:

- First circle and play each **6th**.
- Then play *Taps,* using the pedal.

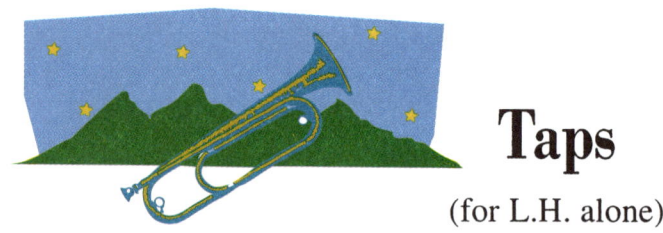

Taps

(for L.H. alone)

U.S. Army Bugle Call

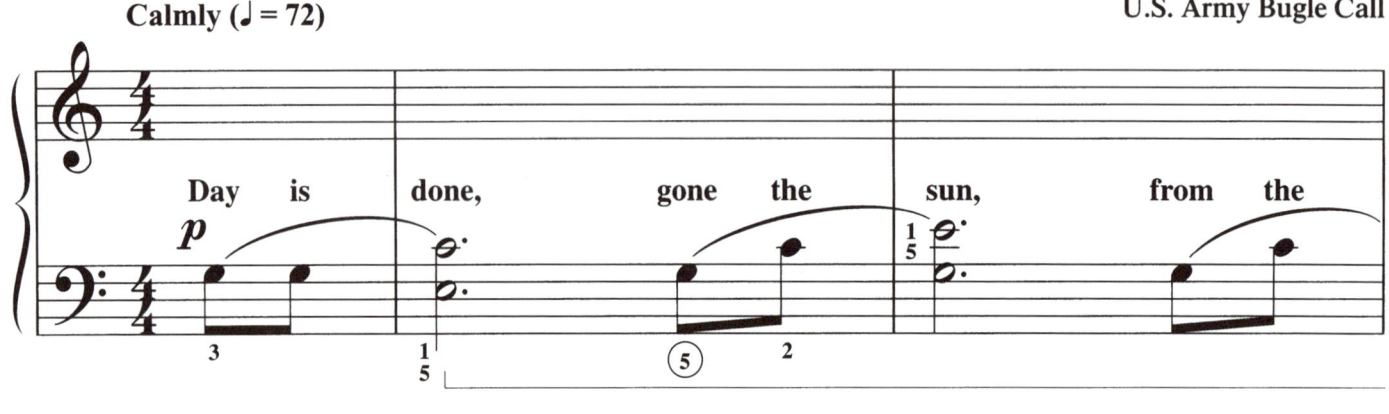

Compose a short melody for the left hand that uses 6ths.

1st and 2nd endings

|1. |2.

Play the 1st ending and take the repeat.
Then play the 2nd ending, skipping over the 1st ending.

Shave and a Haircut

Traditional

(music score: Fast and happy, mf, with 1st and 2nd endings; lyrics under 2nd ending: "Shave and a hair-cut, two bits!" with f dynamic and (prepare L.H.) notation)

DISCOVERY

Identify each L.H. rest in the last line of music.

The C Major Scale ✓

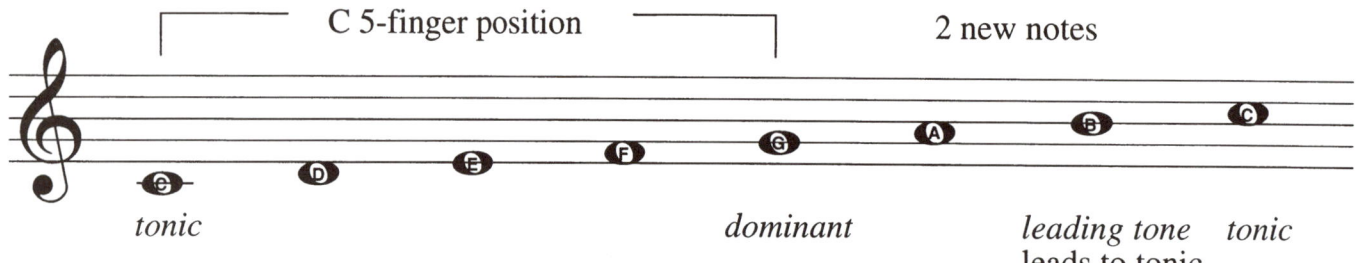

The C major scale is the C 5-finger position plus two added notes (A and B).
All seven letters of the musical alphabet are used in a major scale.

In the Key of C:
The 1st tone, **C,** is the **tonic**.
The 5th tone, **G,** is the **dominant**.
The 6th tone, **A,** is a whole step above the dominant.
The 7th tone, **B,** is the **leading tone**. It is a half-step below C and pulls up to C, the tonic.

Point out the **tonic**, **dominant** and **leading tone** on the staff above. Then find and play them on the piano.

Roadmap for the Key of C

DISCOVERY Your teacher may ask you, "In the Key of C major, play a high **tonic** note," or "play a low **dominant** note," or "play the **leading tone**," etc.

See how quickly you can play each one on the piano.

Warm-ups for the C Major Scale

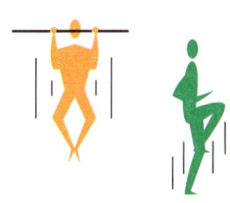

Playing the C Major Scale

Practice slowly and listen for an even tone!
Memorize the fingering for the C major scale.

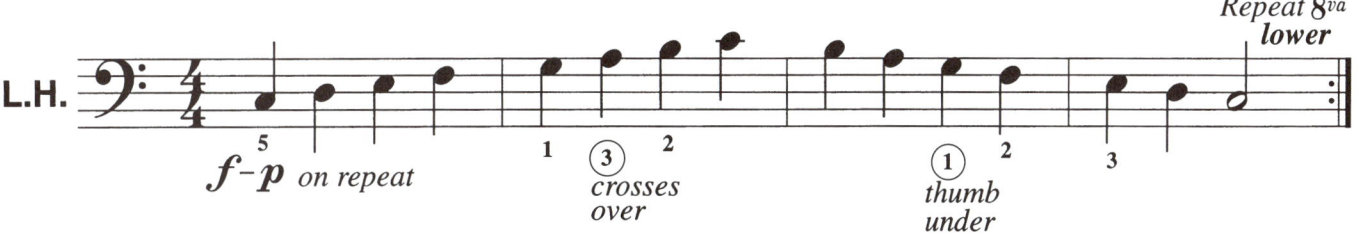

Scale Expert

Put a ☆ in the blank when you can play the C major scale (hands alone) with the metronome ticking at:

legato ♩ = 80 _____   legato ♩ = 104 _____   legato ♩ = 138 _____

staccato ♩ = 80 _____   staccato ♩ = 104 _____   staccato ♩ = 138 _____

Da Capo means the beginning (abbreviated D.C.).
Fine means the end.
D.C. al Fine means return to the beginning and play to *Fine*.

Circle *Fine* and *D.C. al Fine* in this piece.

Jumpin' Jazz Cat

Key of C

Tempo Check: Practice *Jumpin' Jazz Cat* until you can play it at ♩ = 132.

Teacher Duet: (Student plays one octave higher)

DISCOVERY

Point out a descending (going down) C major scale.
Point out an ascending (going up) C major scale.

I and V⁷ Chords in the Key of C

In your earlier lessons you learned a 2-note V7 chord in the Key of C.
To play a 3-note V7 chord, add the *leading tone* (a half step below the tonic).

Practice and memorize these I and V7 chords.

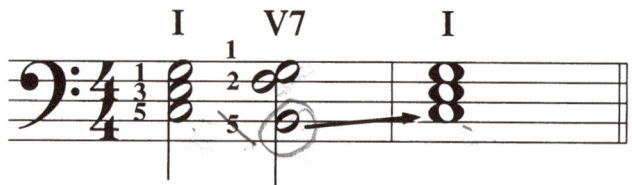

leading tone leads to *tonic*

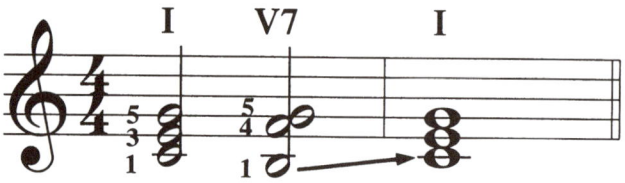

leading tone leads to *tonic*

In this piece, the teacher plays the *melody* (tune).
The student plays the chords or *accompaniment*.

After learning your part well, see if you and your teacher can sing the melody while you *accompany* yourself with I and V7 chords.

Camptown Races Duet

Stephen C. Foster
(1826-1864, American)

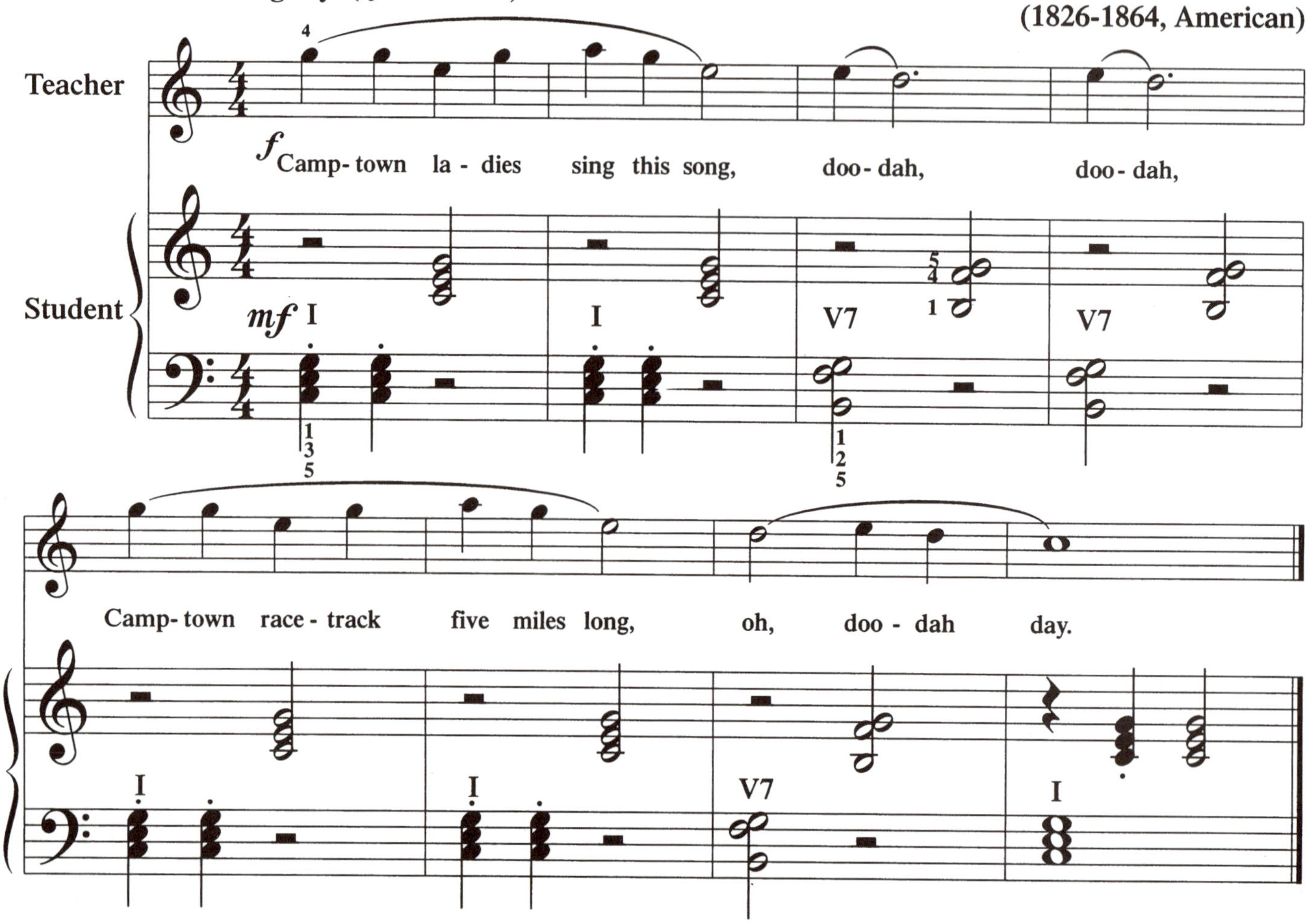

Boom Boom!

Happily ($\quarter = 112\text{-}120$) Traditional

Reading Chord Symbols

Play I and V7 chords in the Key of C by reading the chord symbols below.

Use L.H.   I   V7   I   V7   I   Use R.H.   I   I   V7   V7   I

The Waltz Pattern

A **waltz** is a dance in $\frac{3}{4}$ time.
Here is a popular left hand pattern for a waltz.

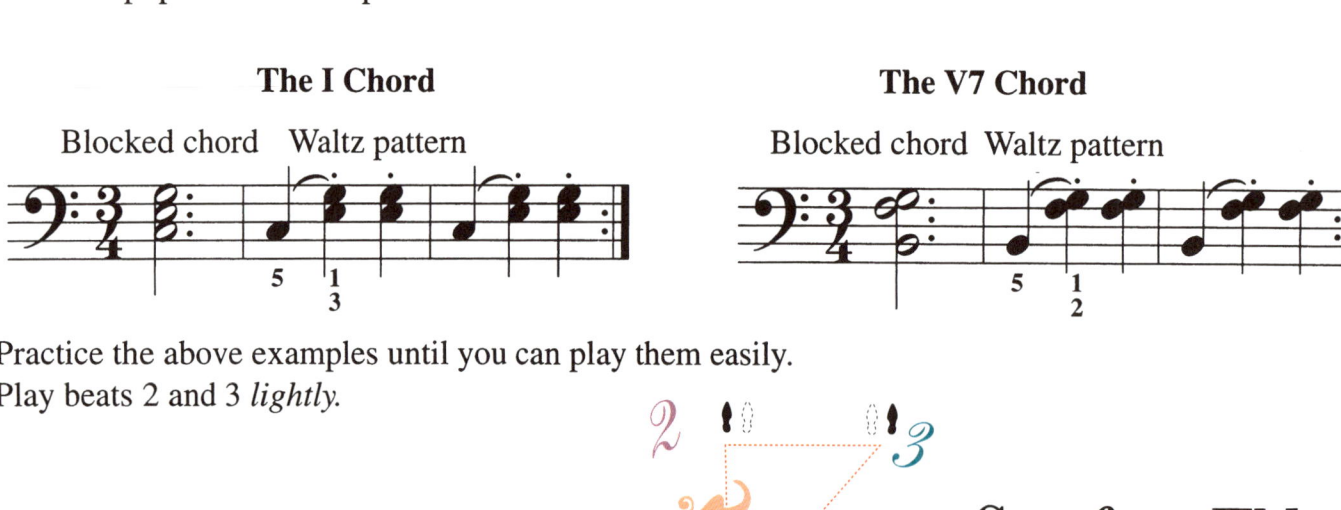

Practice the above examples until you can play them easily.
Play beats 2 and 3 *lightly*.

Carefree Waltz
Key of C Major

With a lilt (♩ = 100-120)

Traditional German

Teacher Duet: (Student plays one octave higher)

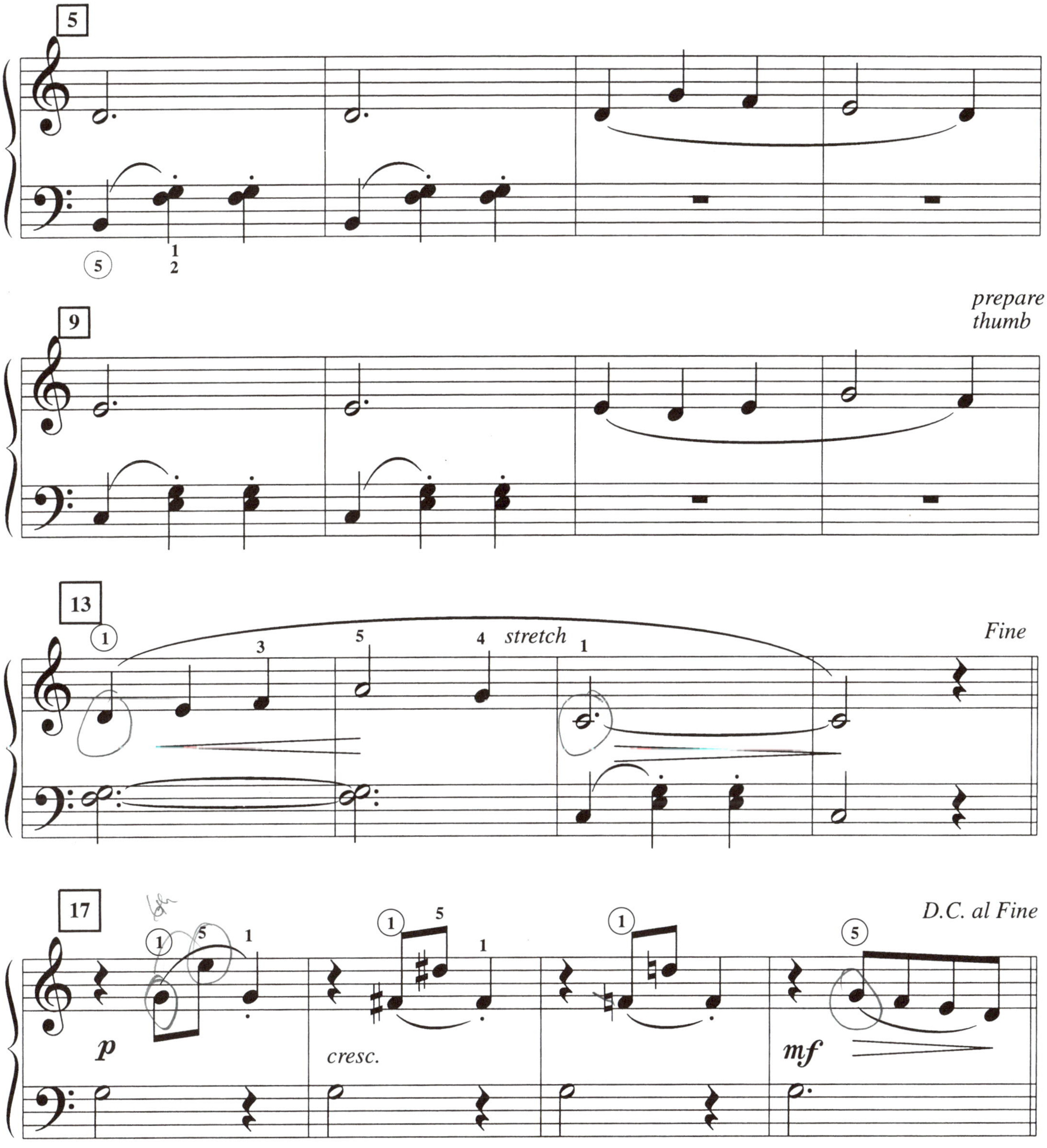

Create a waltz of your own!
Use the L.H. from *Carefree Waltz* and create a new R.H. melody.
Have your waltz end at measure 16.

Call it _____'s Carefree Waltz.
(your name)

The G Major Scale

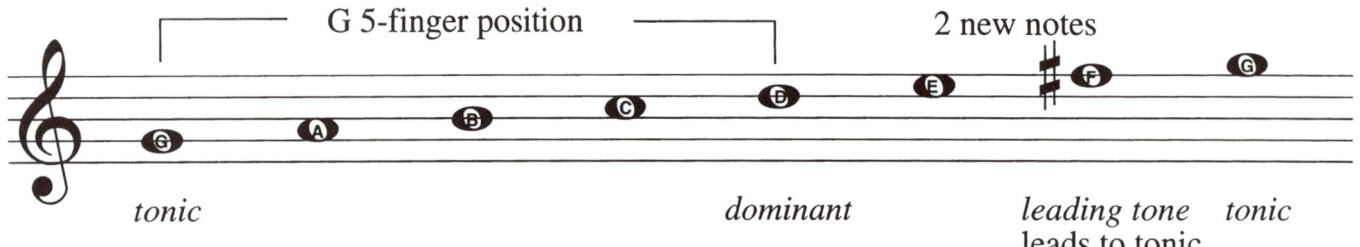

In the Key of G:

The 1st tone, **G,** is the **tonic**.
The 5th tone, **D,** is the **dominant**.
The 6th tone, **E,** is a whole step above the dominant.
The 7th tone, **F♯,** is the **leading tone**. It is a half-step below G and pulls up to G, the tonic.

Find the **tonic**, **dominant** and **leading tone** in the Key of G.

Roadmap for the Key of G

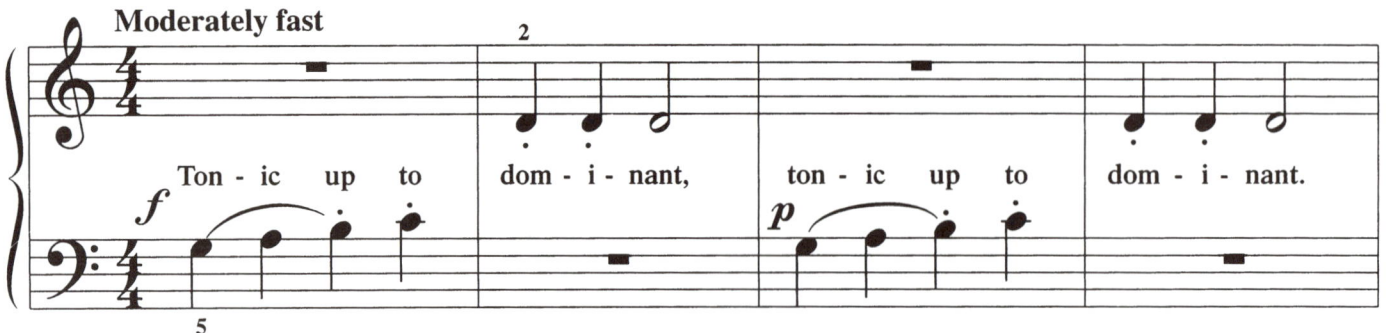

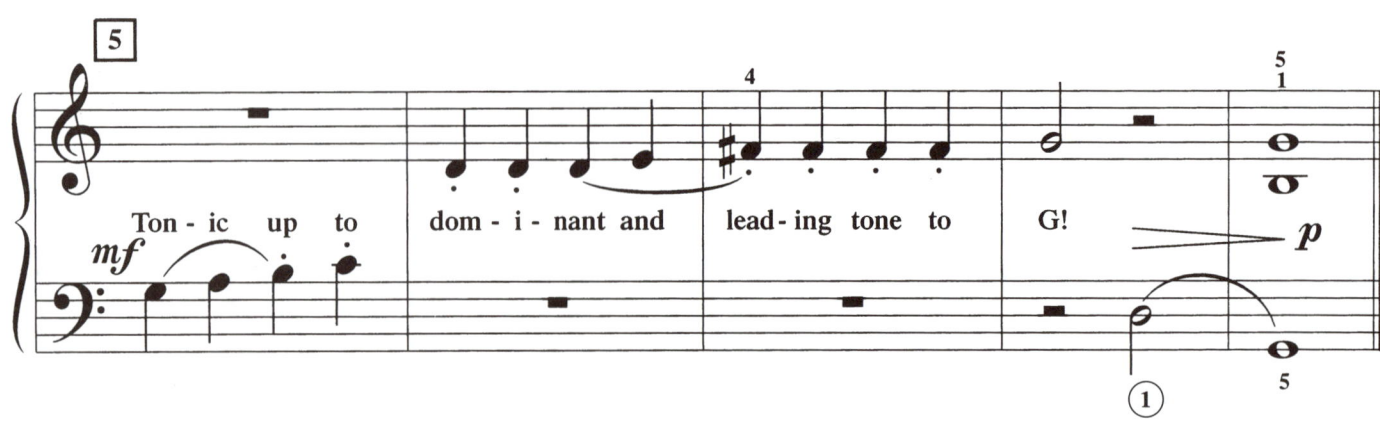

DISCOVERY

See how quickly you can play the **tonic, dominant** and **leading tone** in the Key of G major as your teacher drills you on them.

Warm-ups for the G Major Scale

Playing the G Major Scale

Practice slowly and listen for an even tone!
Memorize the fingering for the G major scale.

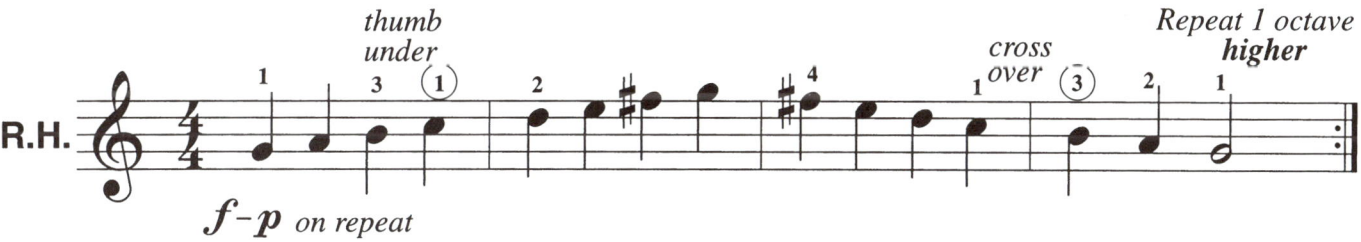

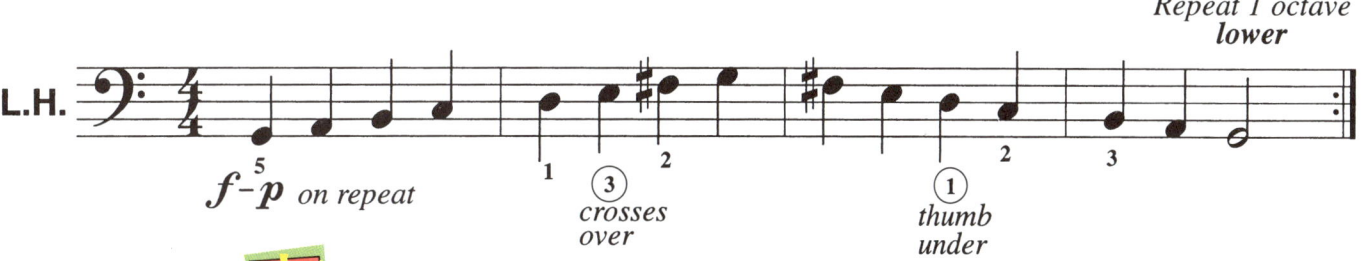

Scale Expert

Put a ☆ in the blank when you can play the G major scale (hands alone) with the metronome ticking at:

legato ♩ = 80 ____   legato ♩ = 104 ____   legato ♩ = 138 ____

staccato ♩ = 80 ____   staccato ♩ = 104 ____   staccato ♩ = 138 ____

Theory p. 17

Review: The G major scale has an F♯.

New: A piece in the Key of G major will also use F♯.

Instead of a sharp before every F, an F♯ is written at the beginning of each staff in the piece. This is called the **key signature**.

Key signature for G major

These sharps mean to play all F's as **F sharp!**

Can you find and circle all the F sharps in *Turkish March*? The first two lines of music have been done for you.

Turkish March

Key signature for G major

Ludwig van Beethoven
(1770-1827, Germany)

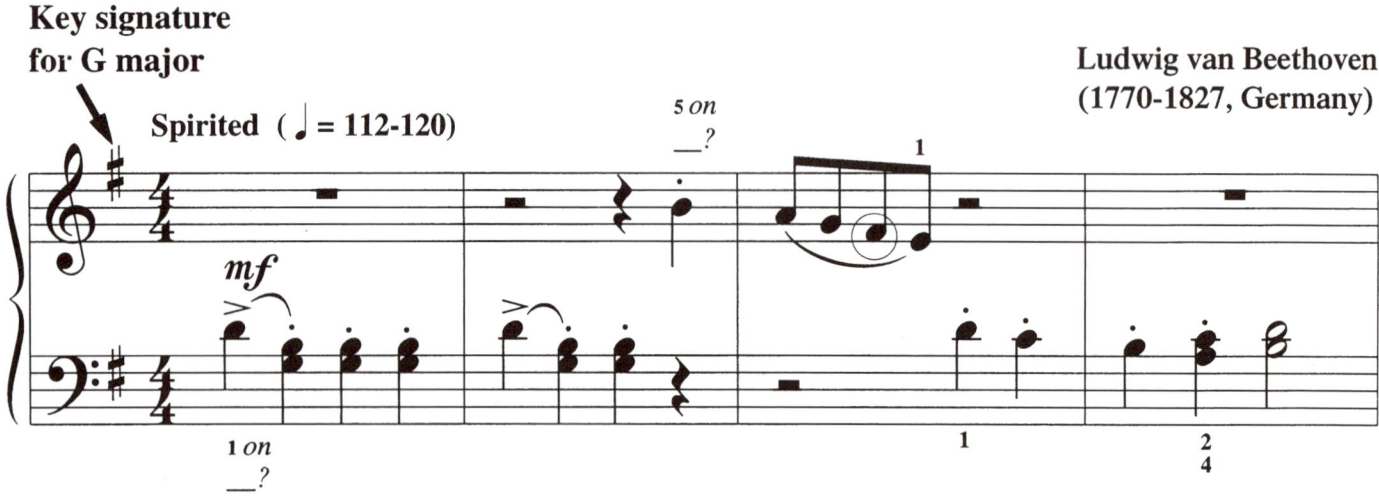

Teacher Duet: (Student plays 1 octave higher)

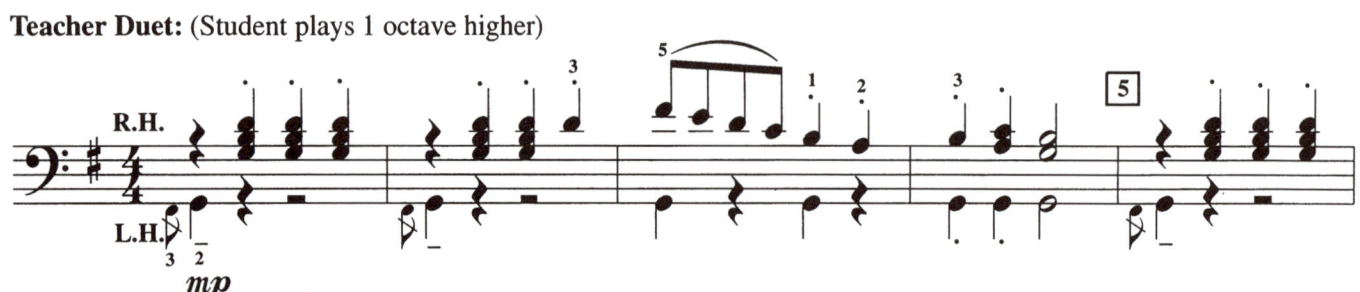

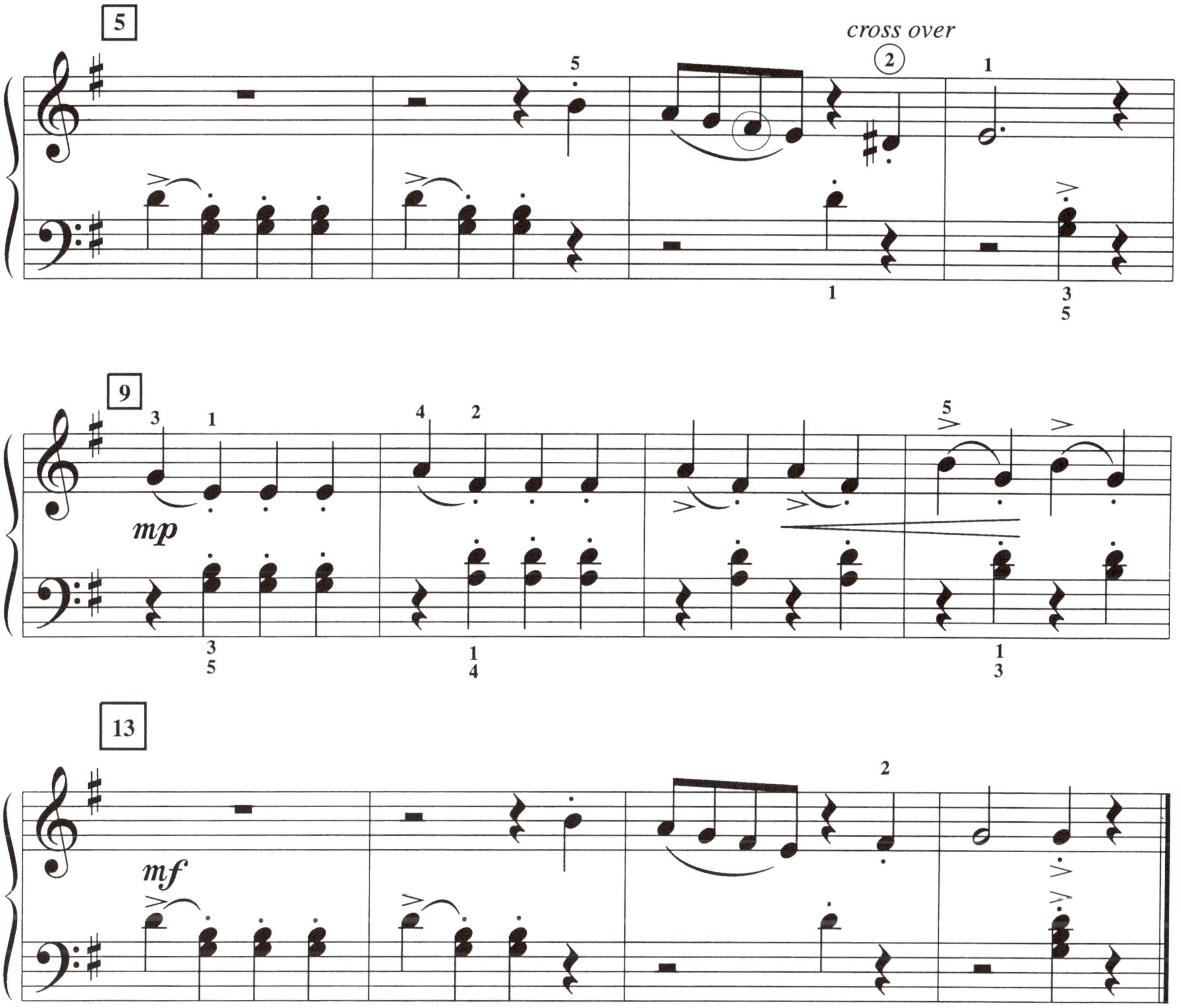

Make up a short L.H. melody in the Key of G.
Be sure to play all the F's as F sharps. Call it *"Submarine."*

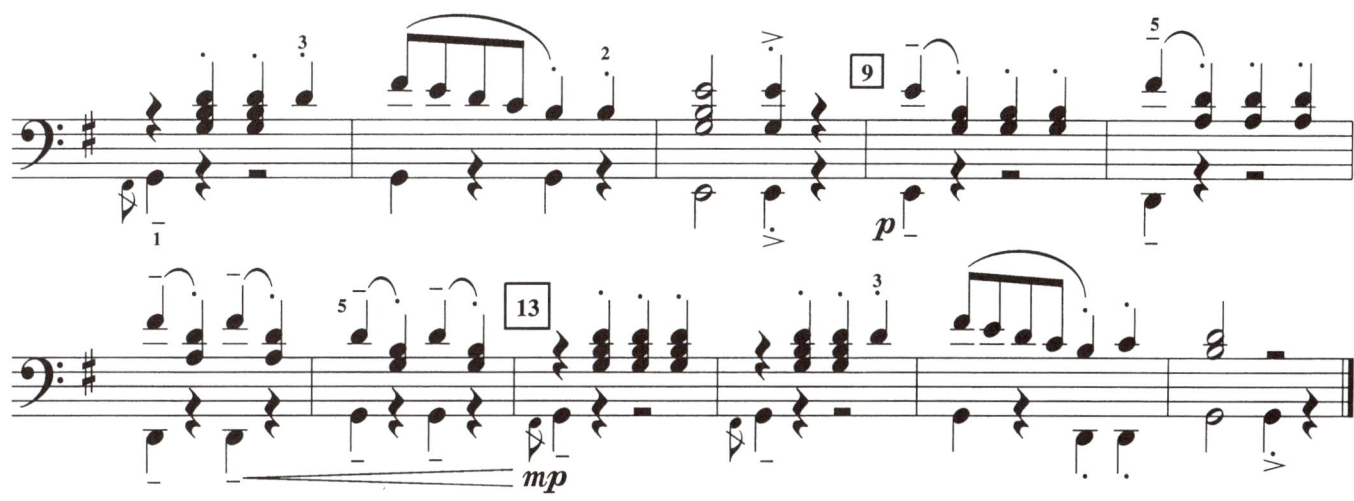

I and V⁷ Chords in the Key of G

In your earlier lessons you learned a 2-note V7 chord in the Key of G.
To play a 3-note V7 chord, add the *leading tone* (a half step below the tonic).

Practice and memorize these I and V7 chords.

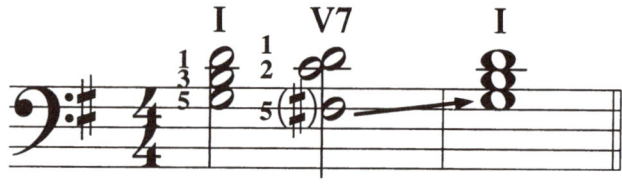

leading tone leads to *tonic*

leading tone leads to *tonic*

Reading Chord Symbols in G

Play the chord patterns below in the Key of G:

Use L.H.   **I   V7   I   V7   I**

Use L.H.   **I   I   V7   V7   I**

Use R.H.   **I   V7   V7   I**

Use R.H.   **I   V7   I   V7   I**

Down By the Bay

In this piece, the L.H. I and V7 chords in the Key of G are used to accompany the melody.

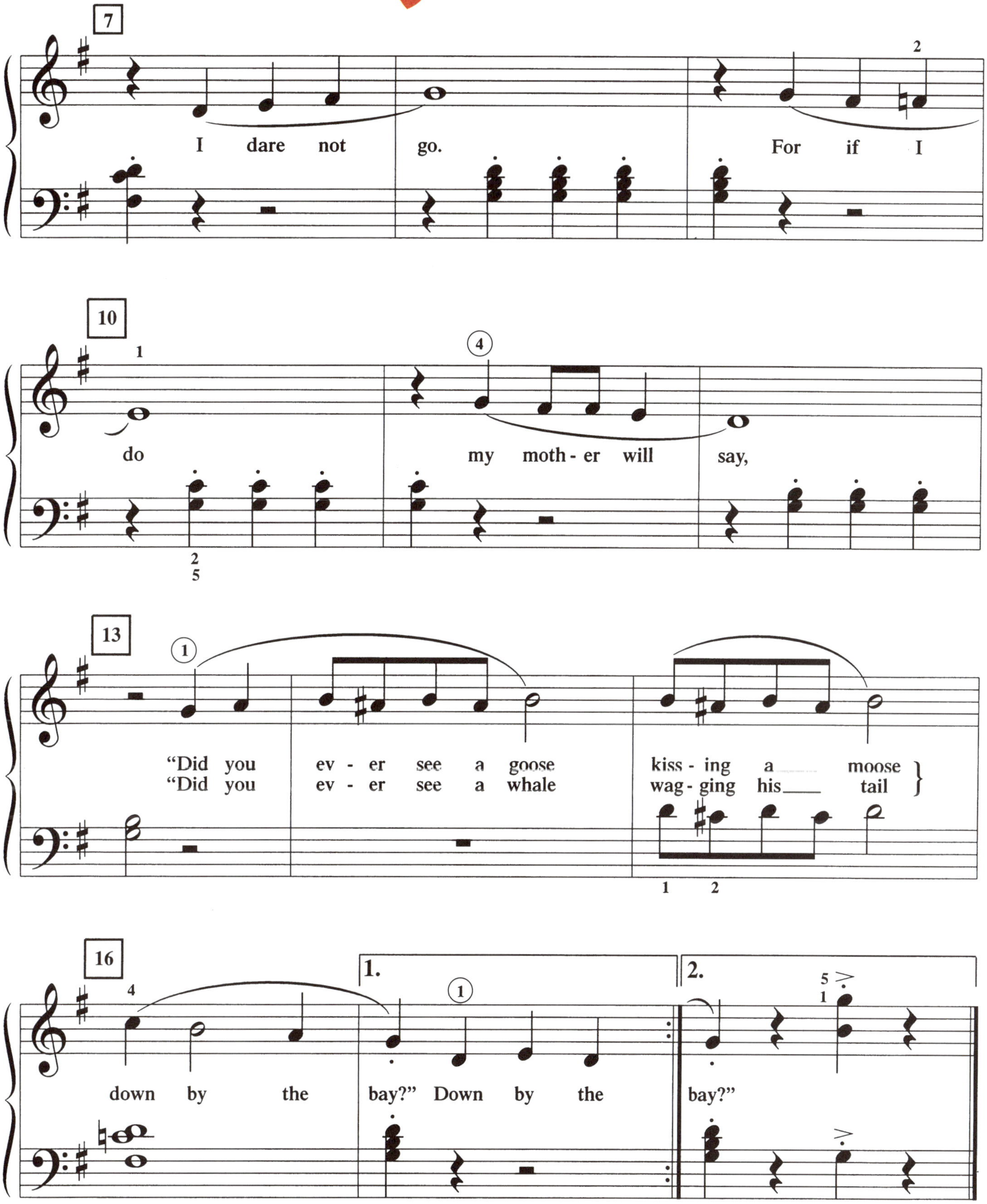

Can you sing the R.H. melody (not play) and accompany yourself by playing the L.H. part? Your teacher may want to sing along with you.

Musical Form

This piece has two parts, the **A Section** and the **B Section**.
Point out these sections in the music below.

This overall plan or **form** is called **AB form**.

Horse Drawn Carriage

Key of _____ Major

Scale Check: Practice until you can play this piece with the metronome ticking at ♩ = 132.

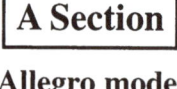

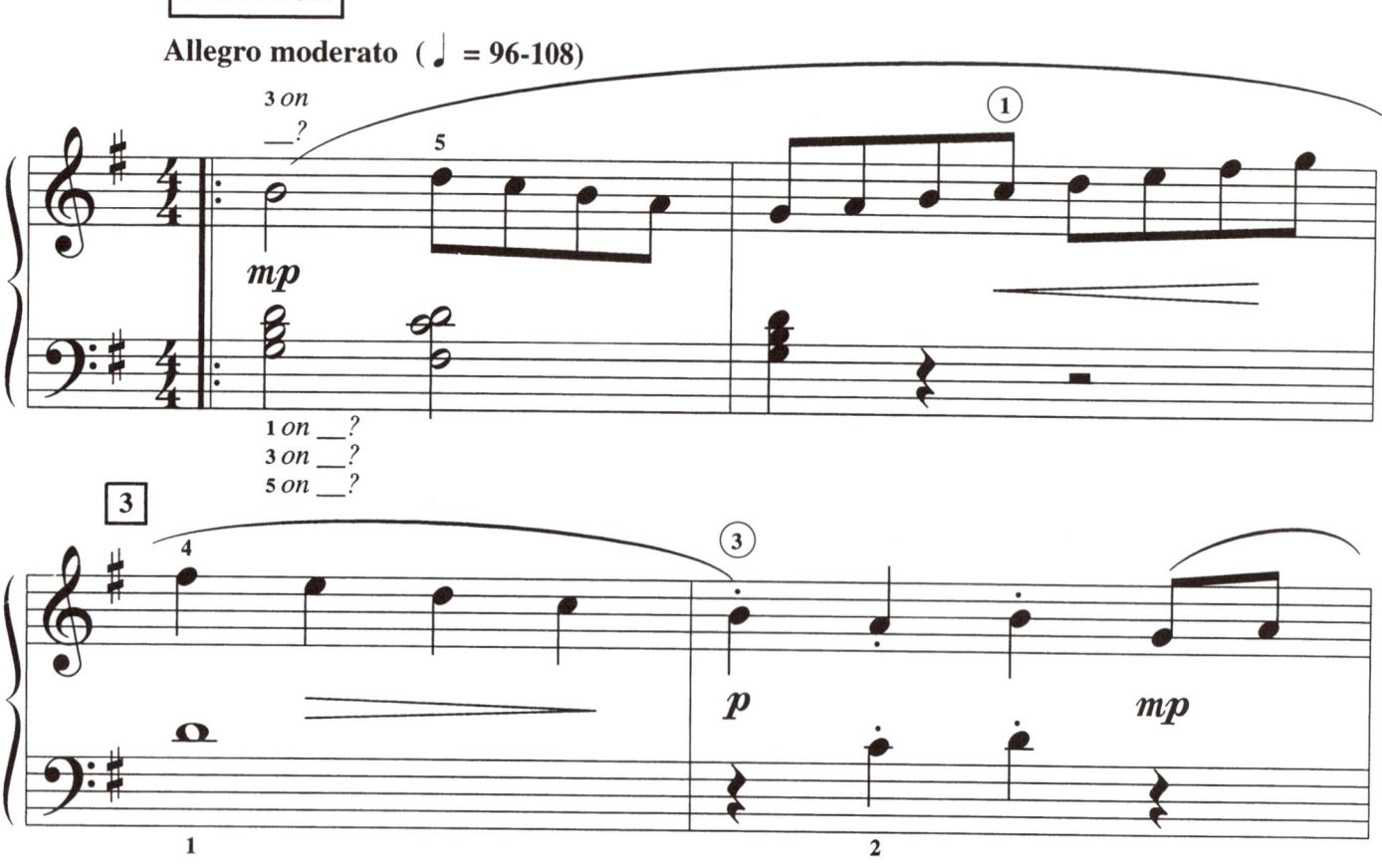

Teacher Duet: (Student plays 1 octave higher)

> Remember that transposition means playing the same music in a different key.
> The note names change, but the intervals stay the same.
>
> Transpose *Horse Drawn Carriage* to the Key of C major.
> Reading the intervals and listening to the sound will help you transpose.

UNIT 6

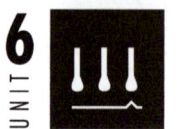

More About the Damper Pedal

The piano has 2 or 3 pedals.

The pedal on the right is called the **damper pedal**.

It is called the damper pedal because it lifts the felts (called dampers) off the strings. This allows the strings to continue to vibrate, which makes the sound ring.

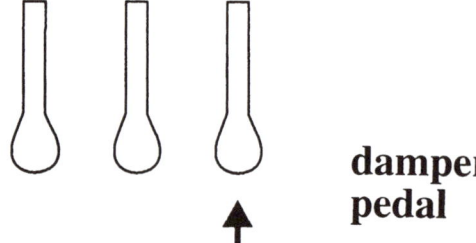

> **Foot Position for the Damper Pedal**
> - Use your right foot.
> - Always keep your HEEL ON THE FLOOR.
> - The toes and ball of your right foot should rest comfortably on the pedal. (Your teacher may wish to demonstrate.)

Pedal Marks

1. Say the words aloud as you pedal this preparatory exercise. Remember your foot position!

   foot
   motion: Up Down Hold it,   Up Down Hold it,   Up Down Hold it,

2. In music, the same foot motion is shown with these pedal marks.
   The ‿ tells you to lift the damper pedal, then depress it again.

   foot
   motion: Up Down Hold it,   Up Down Hold it,   Up Down Hold it,

Technique p. 3 Pedal Pushers, p. 22

First play the R.H. without pedal.

Pedal Hints:

- Say the words aloud as you play *Pedal Power*.
  Notice the pedal goes down AFTER the chord.

- Prepare the next R.H. chord during beats 3 and 4.

- *Listen* carefully for a smooth, connected sound.

Pedal Power

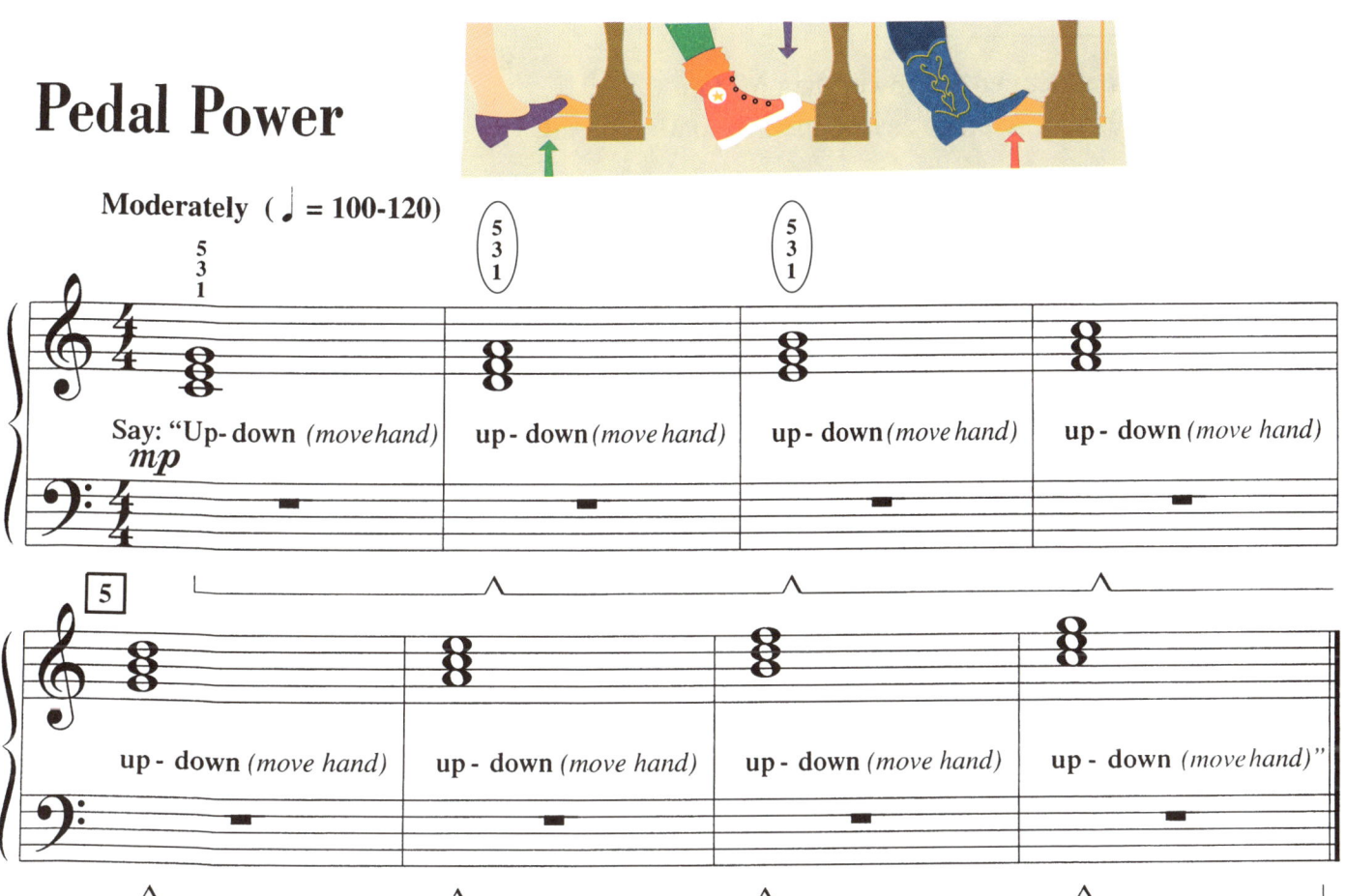

Try playing *Pedal Power* playing **hands together**.
(L.H. plays the same chord 1 octave lower)

Teacher Duet: (Student plays *as written*.)

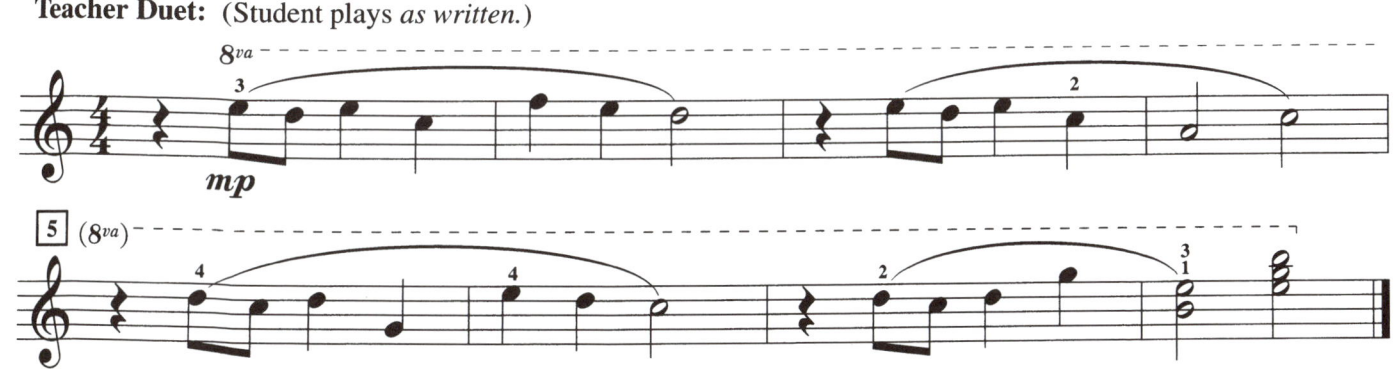

New Note

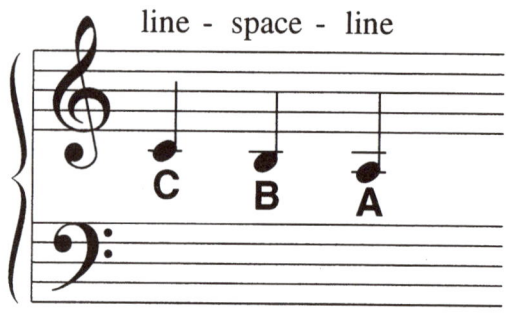

Notice this A is one ledger line lower than Middle C.
Play these 3 notes on the piano saying the note names aloud.

Cover up the notes to the left and quiz yourself by naming these notes.

R.H. Warm-up

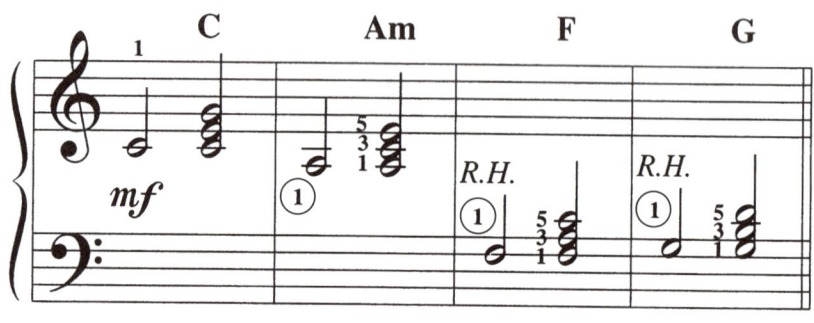

Listen for smooth, connected pedaling!

Beach Party

CREATIVE

1. Make up your own version of *Beach Party*.

   or

2. Play *Beach Party* slowly using **only the L.H.**! (Omit the last L.H. note.)

Teacher Duet: (Student plays *as written*.)

This piece has 3 parts: the **A Section**, the **B Section**, and the return of the **A Section**.

The form of this piece is **ABA**.

Riding the Wind

A Section

Moving freely, with expression (♩ = 104-132)

(prepare L.H.)

Performance p. 14   Theory p. 23   Technique p. 24

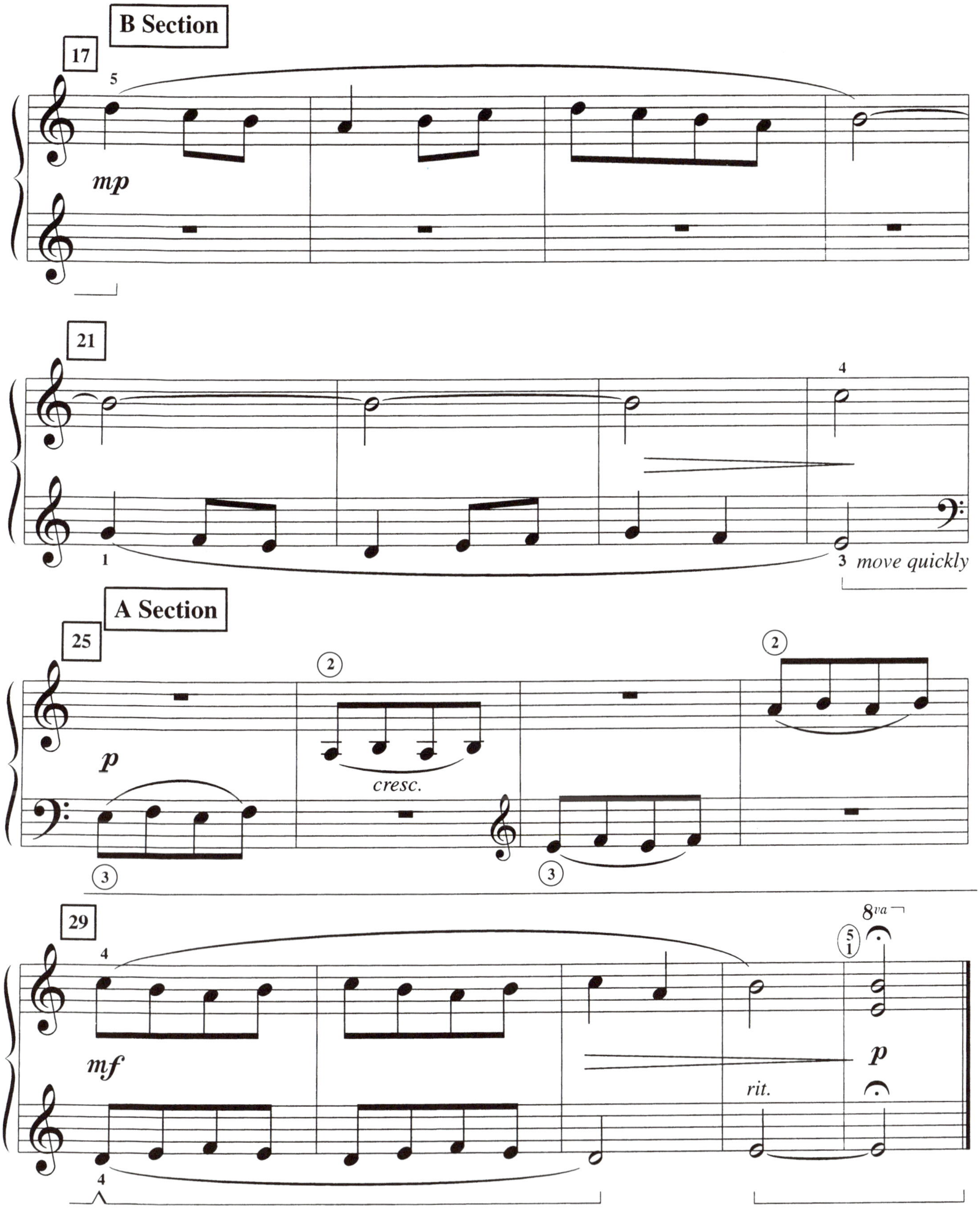

Your teacher may ask you to play this piece at a slower tempo, counting aloud "1 and 2 and." (You are dividing each beat into two equal parts.)

UNIT 7

The Eighth Rest ⁊

eighth note ♪ = one half beat   eighth rest ⁊ = one half beat

Tap this rhythm with your teacher while counting aloud "1 and 2 and."
Notice that each beat is divided into two equal parts.

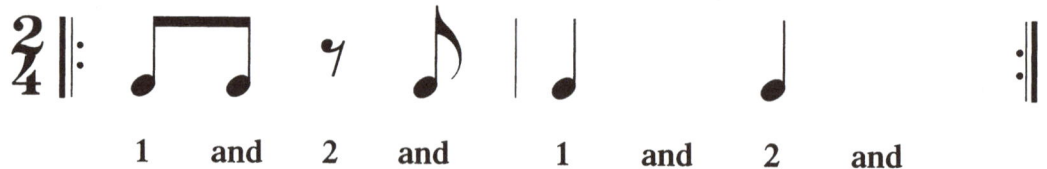

Now tap the rhythm above at these 3 tempos on the metronome:

♩ = 80   ♩ = 96   ♩ = 112

Pumpkin Boogie

The teacher may wish to demonstrate the rhythm in measures 5-6 at ♩ = 144.

Jiving along at a moderate speed

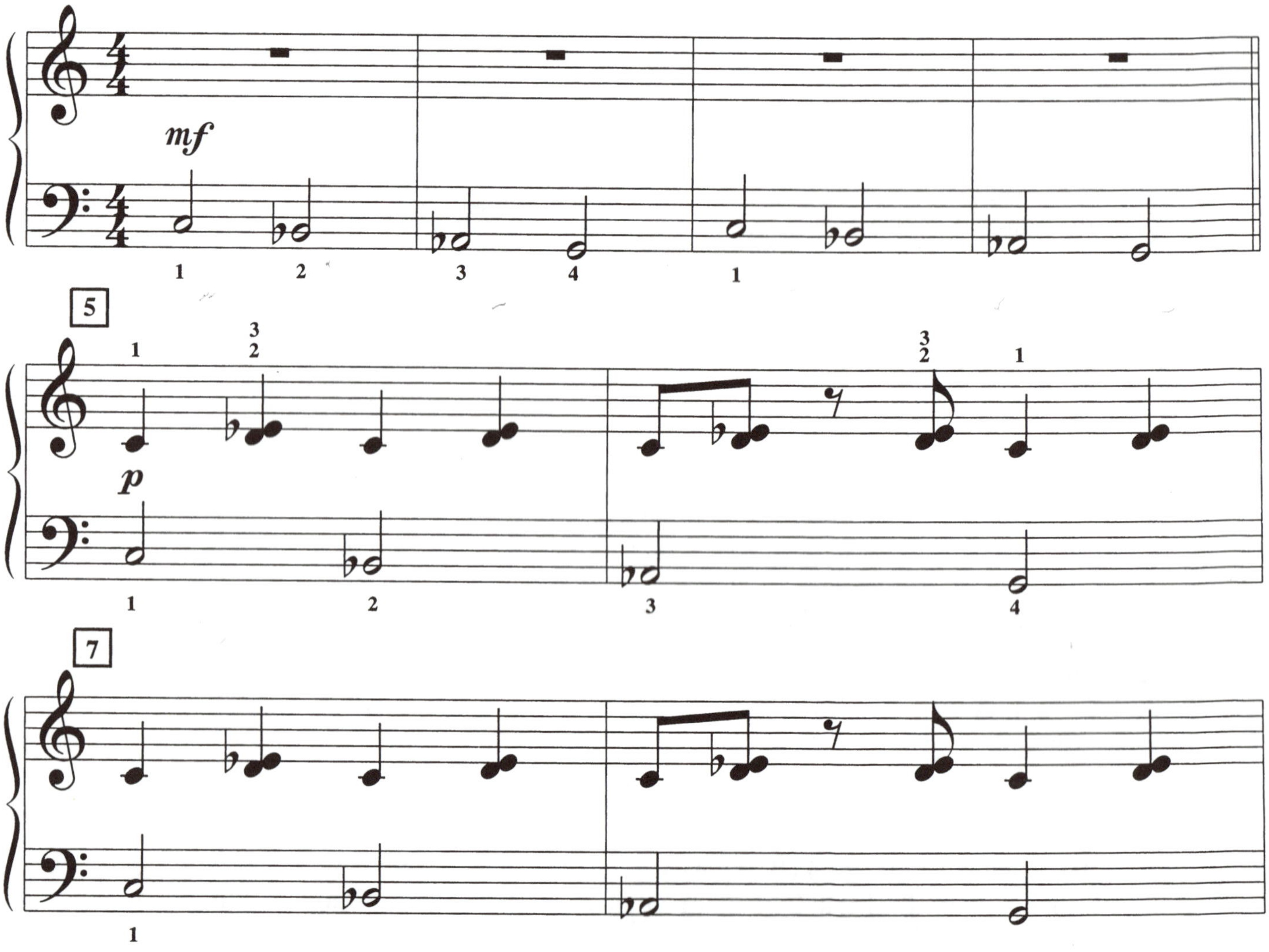

DISCOVERY

Point out the following rests: eighth rest, quarter rest, half rest, whole rest.

UNIT 8

The Dotted Quarter Note

With your teacher, tap the rhythms below on the closed piano lid. Use both hands.
Practice suggestion: Tap the rhythms again with the metronome set at ♩ = 88.

a. [rhythm example in 2/4]
1 (and) 2 and   1 (and) 2 and   1 (and) 2 and   1 (and) 2 (and)

Now **tie** the first 8th note. *Feel* the tied note on beat 2.

b. [rhythm example in 2/4 with ties]
1 (and) 2 and   1 (and) 2 and   1 (and) 2 and   1 (and) 2 (and)

Below, a **dot** replaces the **tied eighth note** used in the example above.
Feel the dot on beat 2! Rhythms **b** and **c** should sound *exactly* the same.

c. [rhythm example in 2/4 with dotted quarters]
1 (and) 2 and   1 (and) 2 and   1 (and) 2 and   1 (and) 2 (and)

(Your teacher may suggest other ways for you to count the ♩. ♪ rhythm.)

London Bridge

Key of _____ Major

Very steady beat

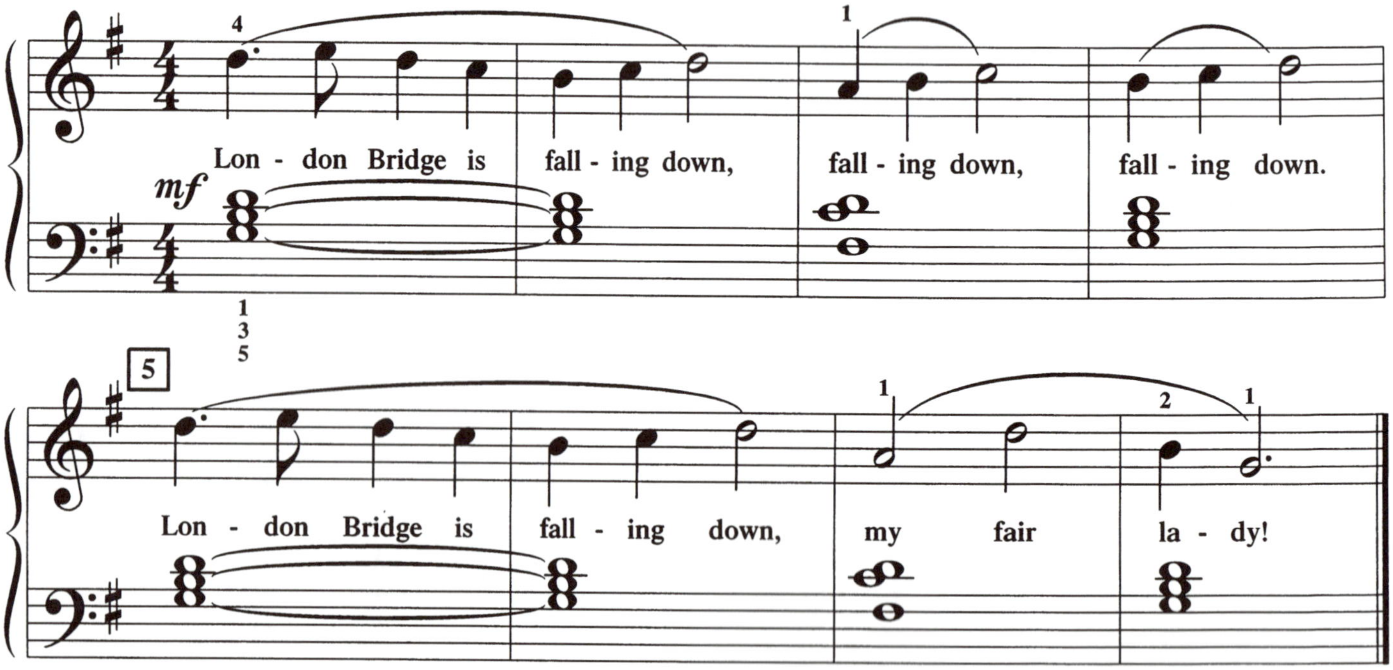

[Sheet music for London Bridge]

Lon - don Bridge is | fall - ing down, | fall - ing down, | fall - ing down.

Lon - don Bridge is | fall - ing down, | my fair | la - dy!

DISCOVERY

Transpose *London Bridge* to the Key of C. (The R.H. finger 4 begins on G.)

America

Key of _____ Major

This piece uses the ♩. ♪ rhythm in 3/4 time.
Feel the dot on beat 2.

Samuel F. Smith

Majestically

mf My coun-try 'tis of thee, sweet land of lib-er-ty,

of thee I sing. Land where my fa-thers died,

land of the pil-grim's pride. From ev-ery___
cresc.

thumb under
moun-tain-side, let___ free-dom ring!
rit. *f*

Performance p.18   Theory p.28   Technique p.29

DISCOVERY

Circle the following for the left hand:
V7 chord in the Key of C, an eighth note, a ledger line C, a C major chord.

Review: The key signature for C major has no flats or sharps.

New: Flats or sharps that are written in the music but are not in the key signature are called **accidentals**. A *natural* is also an accidental.

Notice the B♭ accidental in measure 2.
How many accidentals are in the last measure? ____

New Orleans Celebration

Rhythm Check: With your L.H., tap the rhythm for measures 1-4.
Keep the beat steady and *feel* the dot on beat 2.

Moderately, with a strong beat (♩ = 96-108)

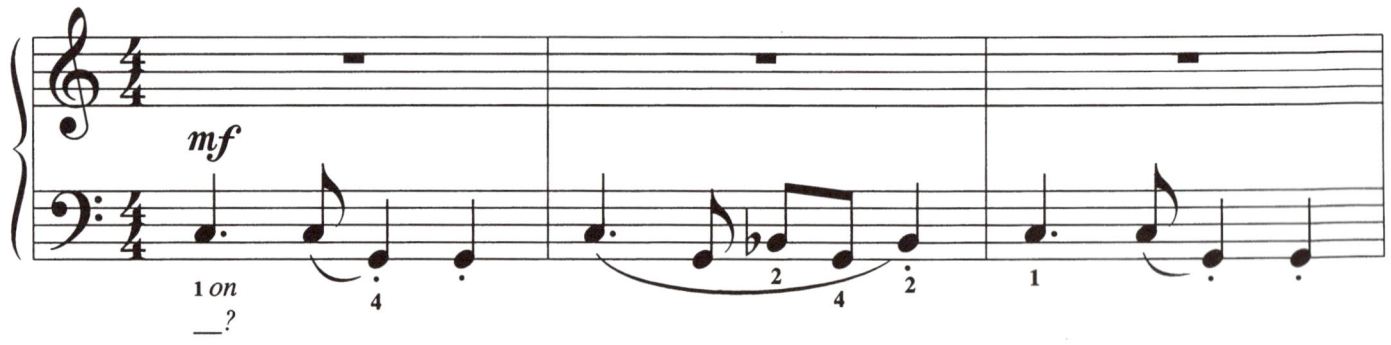

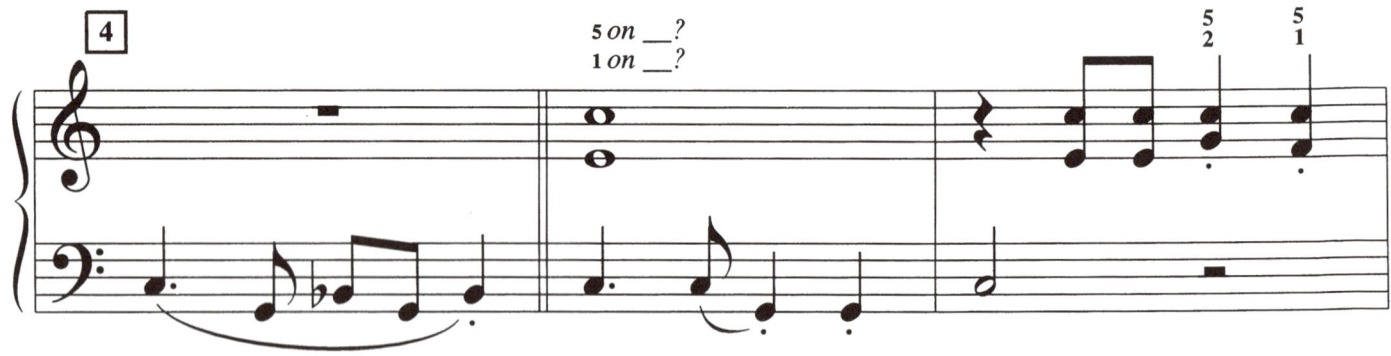

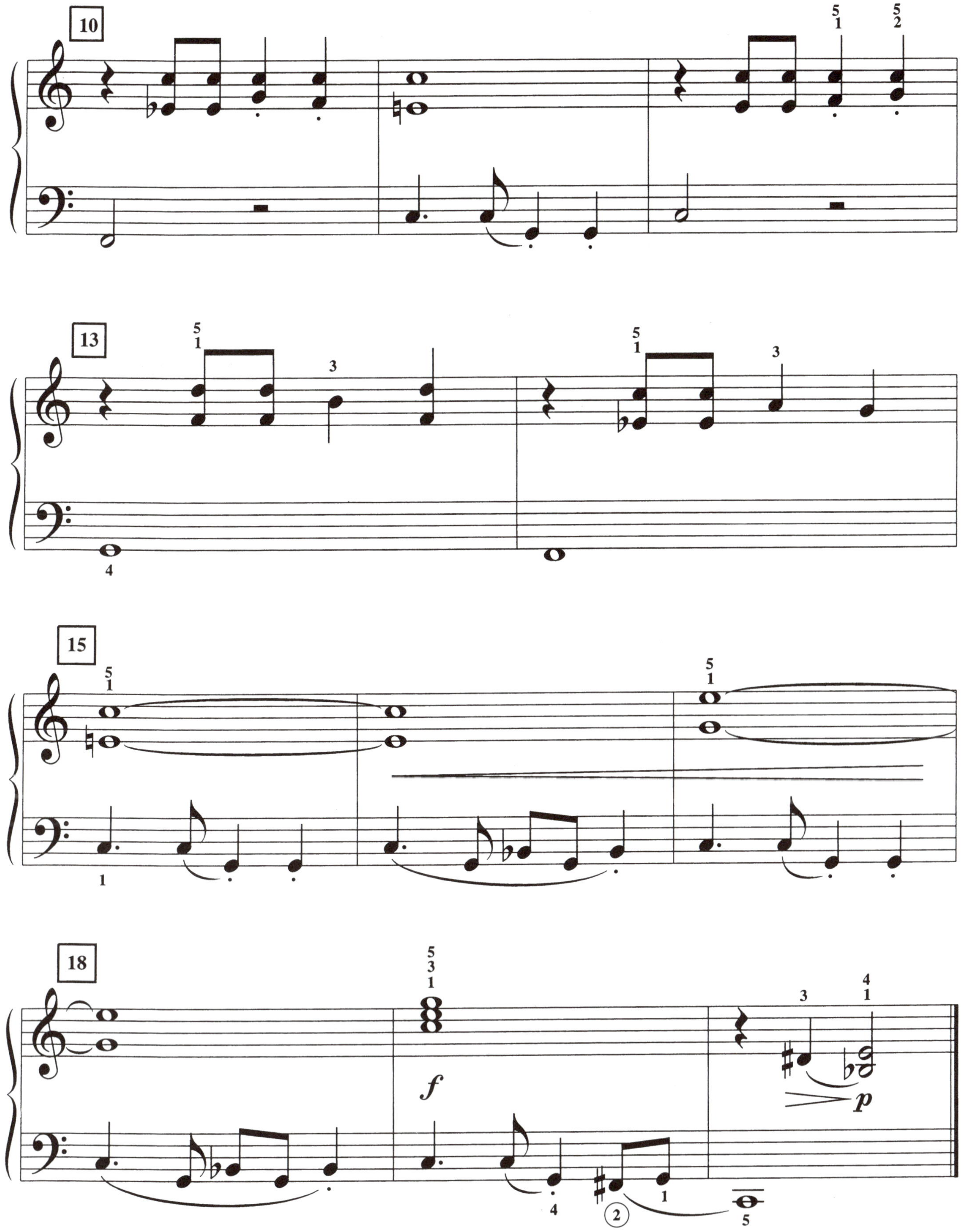

Compose a short piece in the Key of C major that uses one or more **accidentals**.
Call it "Accidentally on Purpose" or a title of your choice.

UNIT 9 — I IV V7

The Primary Chords

are

I   **IV**   **V7**
("one")   ("four")   ("five-seven")

These 3 chords are the primary (most important) chords used with the major scale.
They are built on the first, fourth and fifth tones (steps 1, 4, 5) of the scale.

Watch and listen as your teacher plays the I, IV, and V7 chords in the Key of C.

Chord Drill: Watch the keyboard as your teacher plays one of the chords above in the key of C major.
Say aloud, "I chord," "IV chord" or "V7 chord," depending on what is played.

Chord Jumps

Key of C Major

Practice *Chord Jumps* saying the words aloud.

Lively

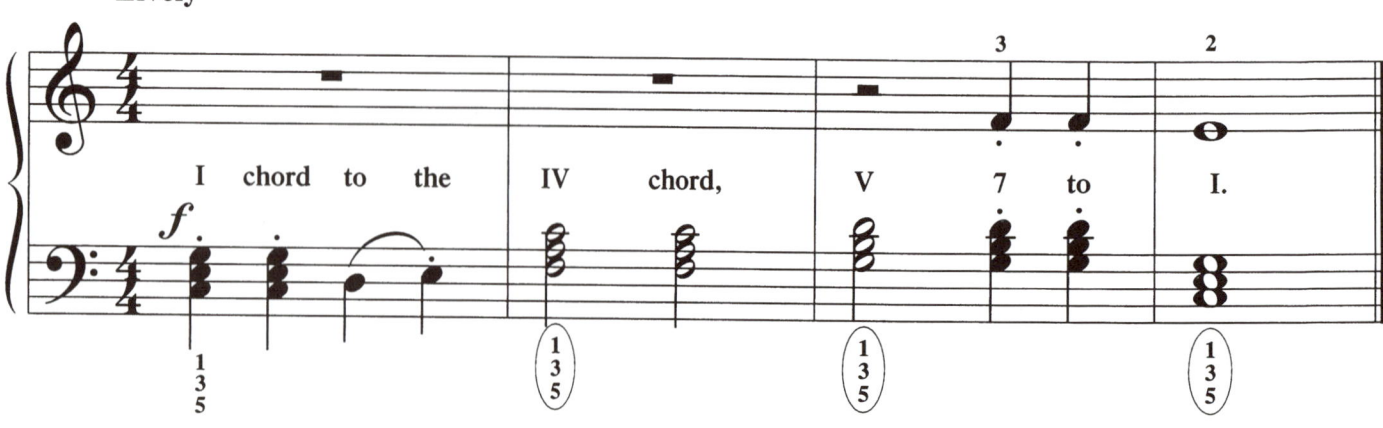

DISCOVERY

Write the letter names of the **I** chord. ___ ___ ___

Write the letter names of the **IV** chord. ___ ___ ___

Write the letter names of the **V7** chord. ___ ___ ___ ___

Did you notice how much jumping the L.H. did in *Chord Jumps*?
By rearranging the notes, the same chords can be played more smoothly.

Helpful Hints:

To play the L.H. IV chord —
- Finger 5 stays in the 5-finger pattern
- Finger 2 stays in the 5-finger pattern
- The thumb moves UP a whole step

I   IV   I
(still F - A - C
but rearranged)

Lazy Chord Blues

Key of C Major

Practice Hints:

1. Practice L.H. alone, without pedal.
2. Practice L.H. with pedal.
3. Now play hands together.

Write **I**, **IV**, or **V7** for each measure.

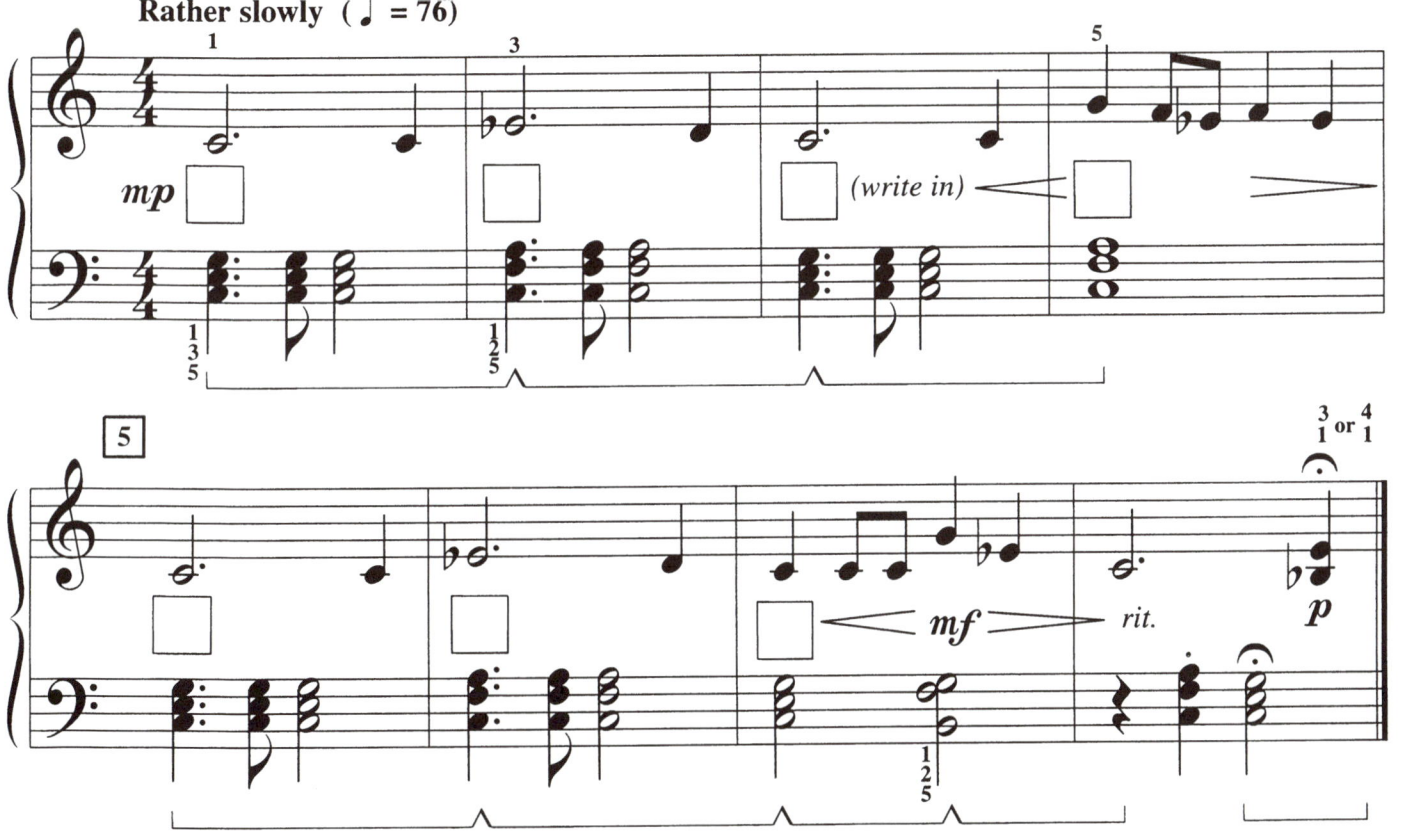

*The Slavic composer Dvořák wrote this famous theme for his *Symphony No. 9*,
'*From the New World.*' "The New World" refers to America in the late 1800's.

Reading Chord Symbols

Play I, IV and V7 chords in the Key of C by reading the chord symbols below.

L.H. I IV I IV I   R.H. I I IV IV I

L.H. I IV I V7 I   R.H. I IV I V7 I

I, IV and V⁷ Chords in the Key of G

Say the chord symbols aloud as you play each chord. Notice the fingering.
Practice and memorize the I, IV and V7 chords in the key of G.

I   IV   I   V7   I

I   IV   I   V7   I

Reading Chord Symbols

Play the chord patterns below in the Key of G. Play the L.H. and then the R.H.

I	I	IV	IV	I		
I	IV	I	IV	I	V7	I
I	V7	I	IV	I	V7	I

The Duke of York

Wrist Check: This piece has many repeated notes.
Play them with firm fingertips, but with a loose, relaxed wrist.

Traditional

DISCOVERY

Which hand has the accompaniment? ____ the melody? ____
Transpose the *Duke of York* to the Key of C. The L.H. will begin on Low C.

New Dynamic Sign

pp — *pianissimo*

Pianissimo means very soft, softer than *piano*.

In this G major piece the notes of the I, IV and V7 chords are played separately.

Combining broken chords with pedal creates a lovely sound on the piano.

Canoeing in the Moonlight

Key of _____ Major

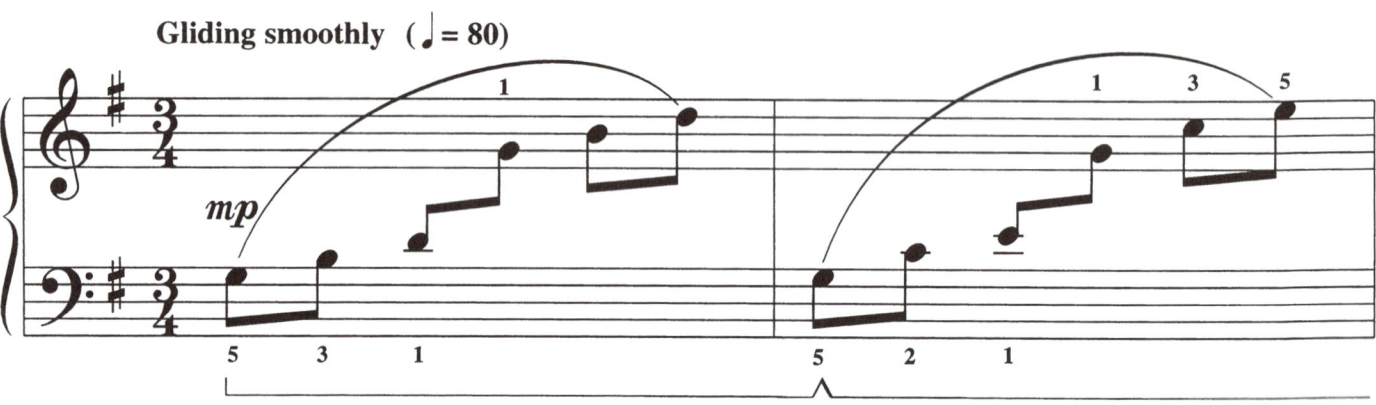

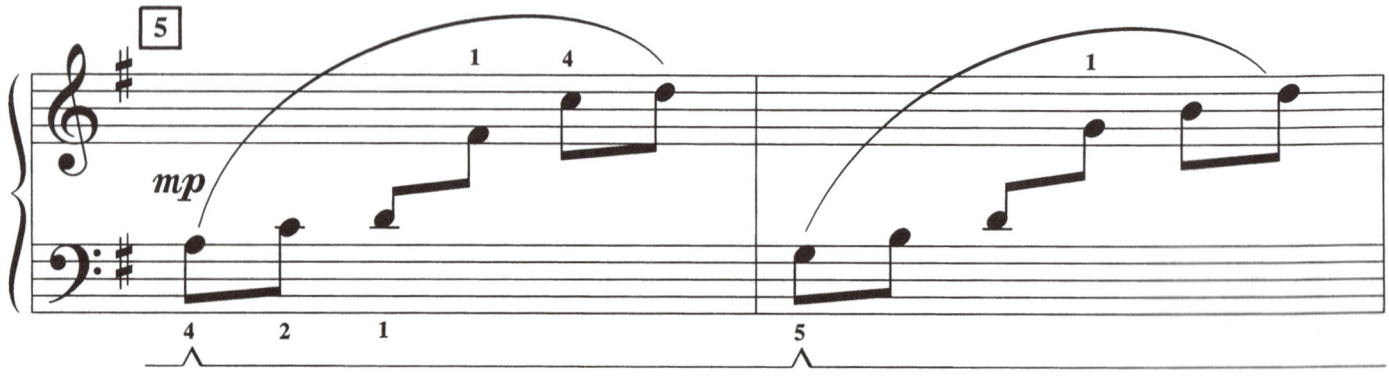

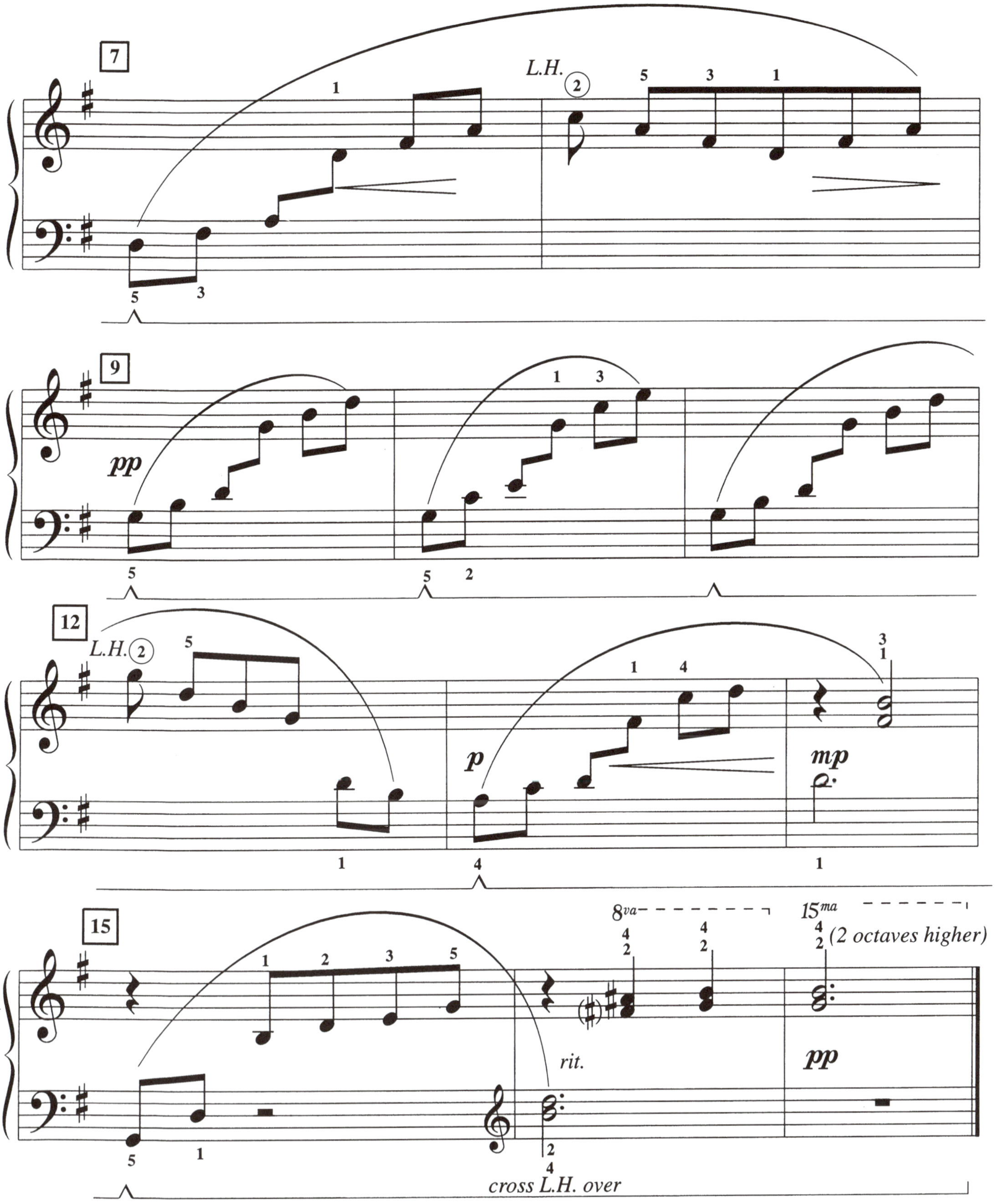

Compose your own broken chord piece in the Key of G.
Call it "Ripples in the Water" or a title of your choice.

UNIT 10

The F Major Scale

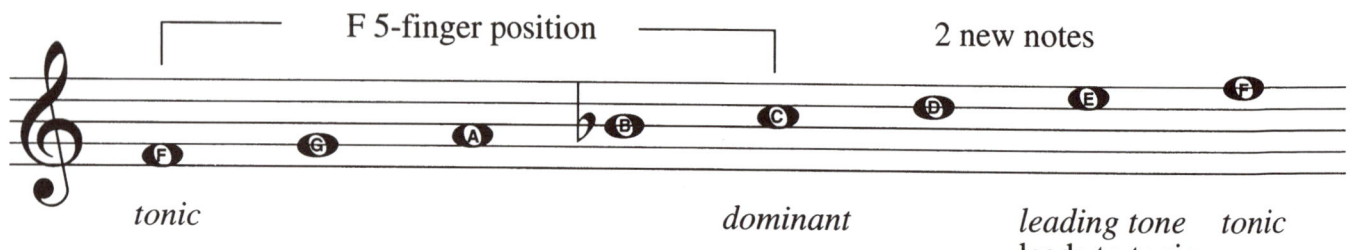

In the Key of F:

Which note is the **tonic**? _____

Which note is the **dominant**? _____

Which note is the **leading tone**? _____

The key signature of F is one flat – B♭.
Circle the key signature for the music below.

Roadmap for the Key of F

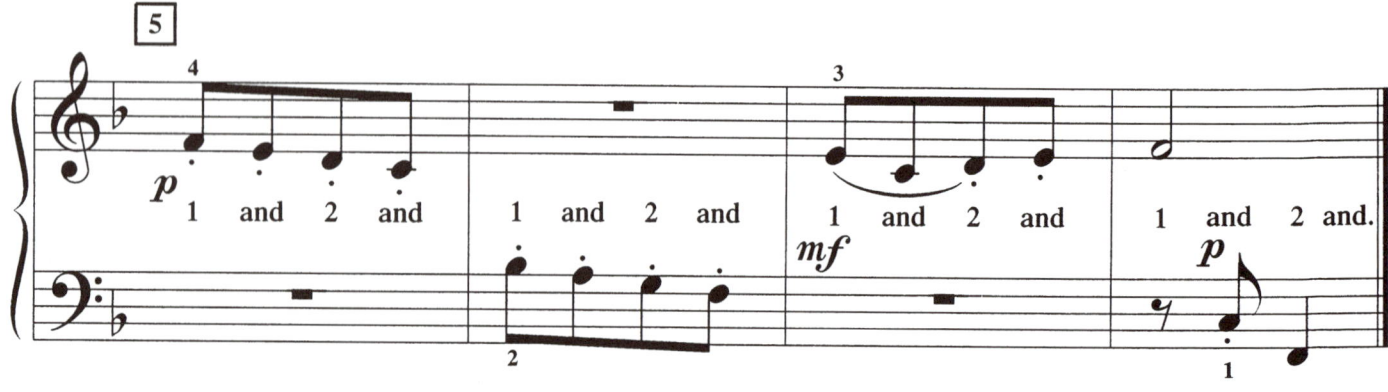

DISCOVERY On the piano, find the **tonic, dominant** and **leading tone** in the Key of F as your teacher calls for each one.

Warm-ups for the F Major Scale

Playing the F Major Scale

Practice slowly and listen for an even tone!
Memorize the fingering for the F major scale.

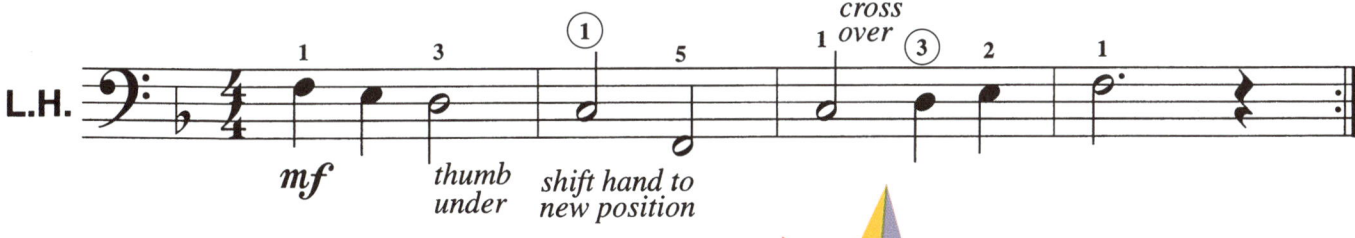

The L.H. fingering for the F scale is the same as the L.H. fingering for the C and G scales.

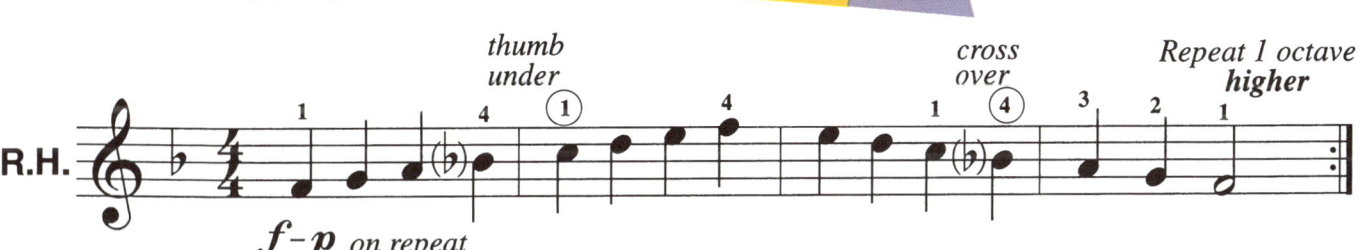

Scale Expert

Put a ☆ in the blank when you can play the F major scale (hands alone)
with the metronome ticking at:

legato ♩ = 80 ____	legato ♩ = 104 ____	legato ♩ = 138 ____
staccato ♩ = 80 ____	staccato ♩ = 104 ____	staccato ♩ = 138 ____

Theory p.37

Amaryllis*

Key signature for F Major
Circle all the B flats in this piece before playing.

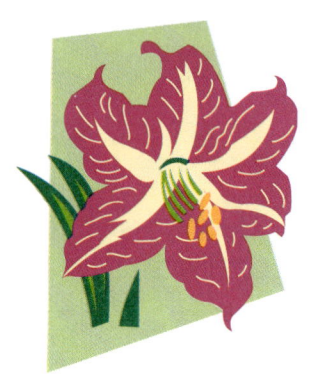

Henri Ghys (France)

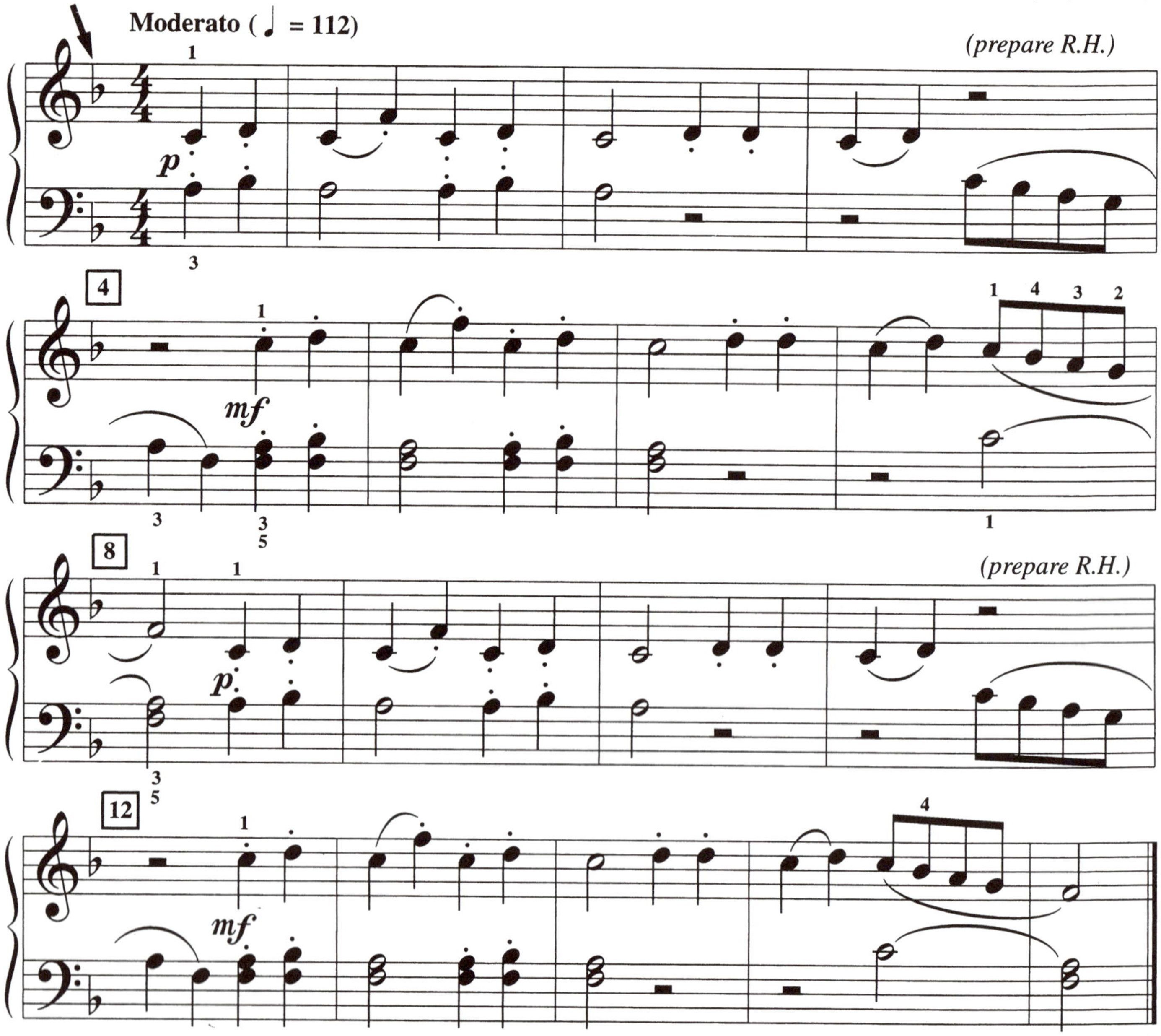

Amaryllis is a plant with clusters of large red, white, purple, or pink flowers.

Teacher Duet: (Student plays 1 octave higher)

Performance p. 26 Technique p. 24

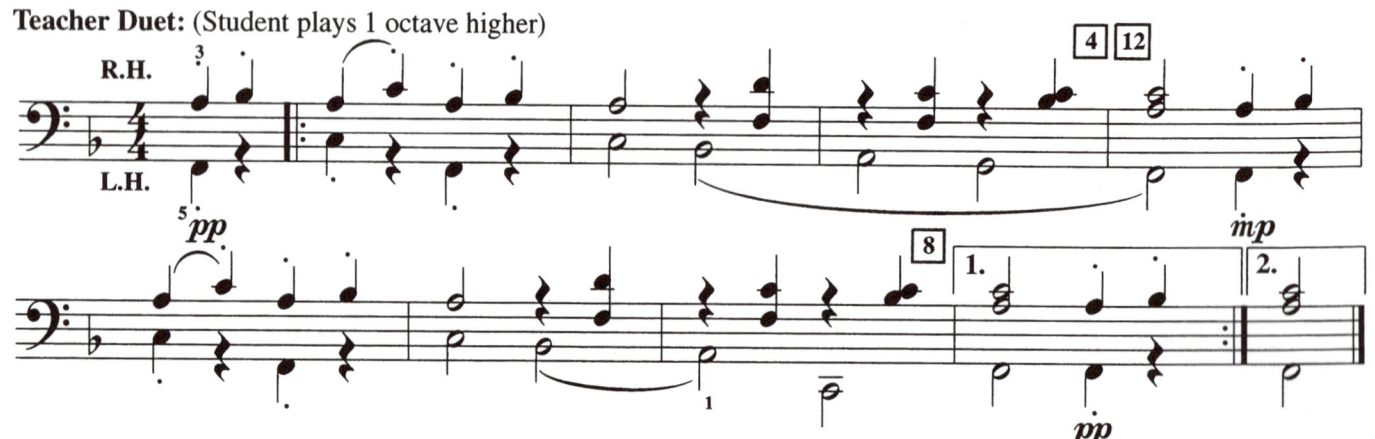

I, IV and V⁷ Chords in the Key of F

Blocked Chords — The chord tones are played together.

Transpose the blocked chords above to the Key of G.

Broken Chords — The chord tones are played separately.

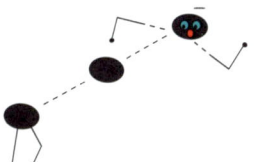

Transpose the broken chords above to the Key of C.

Reading Chord Symbols

Play the chord patterns below in the key suggested.
Use blocked chords, playing hands alone or hands together.

Key of F:	I	I	IV	IV	I	IV	I
Key of G:	I	IV	I	I	V7	V7	I
Key of C:	I	V7	I	V7	I	IV	I

CREATIVE Make up your own broken chord exercise using one of the three chord patterns above.

Auld Lang Syne

Key of _____ Major

Write I, IV or V7 in the boxes below the chords.

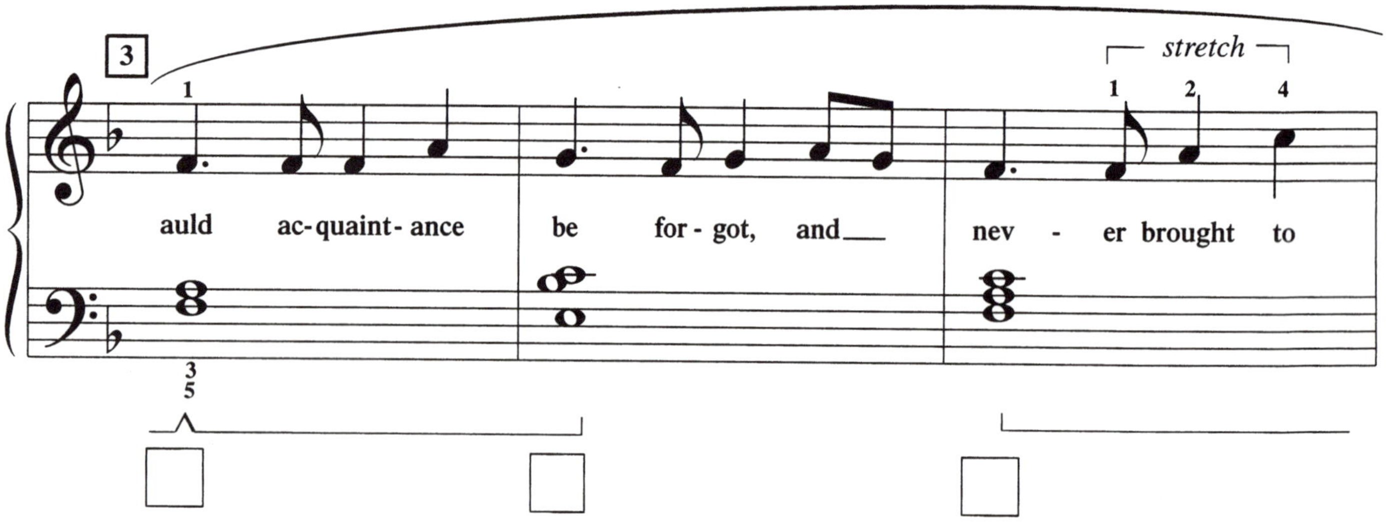

Traditional

Teacher Duet: (Student plays 1 octave higher)

DISCOVERY When you can play *Auld Lang Syne* well in the Key of F major, transpose it to G major. You may begin with the upbeat to measure 3.

Certificate
of Achievement

CONGRATULATIONS TO

_____

(Your name)

You have completed

Piano Adventures® Level 2B

and are now ready for:

Piano Adventures® Lesson Book Level 3A

Piano Adventures® Performance Book Level 3A

Piano Adventures® Theory Book Level 3A

Piano Adventures® Technique & Artistry Book Level 3A

Teacher: _____

Date: _____